SIGNIFICANT RECRUITING

The Playbook for Prospective College Athletes

A step-by-step guide to maximizing your exposure to college coaches at colleges that fit you best

By
Matt Rogers

"A *must-read* book."
- **Jerry Petitgoue**
National High School Coach of the Year

Significant Coaching
Matt Rogers

Published in the United States by Significant Coaching

Editor: Cat Margulis
Cover designed by: Amy Ballantine
Book designed by: Dawn Black
Photos of Matt: Toni Lemma
Additional Graphic Design by Allie Moeller
Cover image: iStock

For more information on the author or this book, visit:
www.significantcoaching.net

Advance Praise
For Significant Recruiting

"This is the playbook every young athlete needs. Developing a strategic plan for the recruiting process is essential, and Matt's book is a detailed outline from someone who knows the process inside and out."

— Lori Chalupny Lawson,
U.S. Women's Soccer World Cup and Olympic Champion

"I can't imagine how daunting the recruiting process must be for parents without their own student-athlete experiences such as mine. Matt's labor of love for young people wanting to achieve their student-athlete dreams shines through in this easy-to-follow recruiting process. It's THE playbook."

- Quinn Wirth,
Former NCAA Division 1 Basketball Player

"This book is a must-read for all parents and prospective student-athletes! I've coached at the collegiate level for nine years and I found it full of insights!"

— Oliver Wiseman,
Head Coach, Benedictine University Women's Basketball

"Coach Rogers has used his vast knowledge and experience as a Head Coach and National Head Scout to write a terrific book about the recruiting process. He provides honest insights and a step-by-step plan that is sure to help the prospective college athlete and their family."

— Dave Kaneshiro,
Head Coach, University of Hawaii-Hilo Women's Basketball

*For **Karen**, **Kaia** and **Kade**,*
without whose love and selflessness
this book could never have been written.

Table Of Contents

Foreword

I have been a coach my entire career in the small towns of Galena, Ill., Lena, Ill., Gratiot, Wis., and for the past 52 years at Cuba City High School in Cuba City, Wis. Coaching in small towns can be a great advantage for a high school coach because of the lack of distractions that coaches in bigger cities must constantly overcome. My players did not have dozens of options for where they could attend high school, nor did they have choices about which coach they wanted to play for or which AAU (Amateur Athletic Union) club they wanted to join. Our small high school program and playing for me was usually their only option, and I would always do all I could to help my players with their next steps after high school. The disadvantage of being a small-town high school coach is the fact that college coaches are not often driving through rural farming communities looking for players.

I never had to worry about a high level of commitment from my players and families because playing on our team in Cuba City, Wis. (population 2,100) meant that they could count on the fact that we were going to consistently compete for a chance to win a State Championship and that was often their best and sometimes only way to be seen by an interested college coach. Over those many years, my teams have won over 1,000 games and three state championships, and I have been very proud to see over 50 of those young men go on to compete at every level of college basketball.

When Matt asked me to read his book and write the Foreword, I was delighted. Not only because Matt Rogers has been a friend and colleague for more than 30 years, but also because this is a **must-read** book. I coached high school basketball for 60 years, and I wish that I would have had this information Matt shares in this book, so I could have provided this level of help and guidance to my players that I am confident would have increased their college options and put them in greater control of their recruitment.

This book includes information that will assist prospective athletes, coaches, teachers and guidance counselors as they move through the maze of college/university preparation and recruitment. As a coach, I never had a recruitment playbook to follow as I tried to assist students who were interested in playing at the next level and trying to earn athletic scholarships. Significant Recruiting fills that void and then some. The "Game Plan" he teaches in Chapter 4 alone is well worth the price of the book. The emphasis on academics stressed in Chapter 3 tells the player clearly that academic preparation is important in this process and may be the difference between playing in college and never playing in college.

I really believe that this book can make a difference in college recruitment planning. It is an easy read with practical information.

Jerry Petitgoue

- Executive Director, Wisconsin Basketball Coaches Association
- 2020 National High School Basketball Coach of the Year
- 2020 Wisconsin Coach of the Year
- 2003 Wisconsin Basketball Coaches Hall of Fame
- 1981, 1991, 1998 Wisconsin State Championships

Introduction

Significant: Having meaning; having or likely to have influence or effect; probably caused by something other than mere chance[1]

I remember being 23 years old and sitting in the audience at a seminar my boss was forcing me to attend at Saint Louis University. I had a lot of work on my plate as the Community Development Coordinator (it was a fancy title for Residence Hall Director of two huge residence hall towers that included all the athletes for a mid-major Division I university), and I was confident I was going to be wasting an hour listening to yet another kumbaya talk on teamwork or communication or understanding the mind of a college student. I was young and impatient, and I went into this presentation with the worst possible attitude and expectation. While I don't remember the speaker's name or 99% of her presentation 25 years later, I do remember the first sentence that came out of her mouth like I heard it yesterday.

---

1   *Merriam-Webster dictionary*

"I want you all to remove the word SUCCESS from your vocabulary and replace it with the word SIGNIFICANT."

The speaker went on to explain her reasoning. According to her, success was a simple concept. Any student could complete a paper for a homework assignment (success!), but very few people put the kind of effort into writing a paper that results in inspiring the reader in some way, or that changes the way the reader thinks about a certain topic. *That's* significant.

Her talk changed the way I thought, and now think, about success. Since then, I've reached for significance, which to me means making a difference for others, over success—just another box checked off.

As an aspiring basketball coach at the time, I immediately translated that philosophy to my sport:

Anyone can walk into a gym, throw a ball up in the air and make a basket—success! But if you put that same person in a gym with a defender in front of them and 2,000 fans in the stands, would they even be able to get a shot off? I wanted to teach my players how to master their craft and how to always be asking, "How can I do it better?" *Significance.*

Significance became an idea that I wanted every young person I encountered to have as a pillar in their growth and education. I knew the concept of significant living could and should translate to their academics, sports, relationships, future jobs, etc. Significance isn't always just putting more effort into a task or following directions perfectly. Significance can mean taking on a task and learning how to do it more efficiently. It can mean taking a problem and thinking out of the box as to the possible solutions for that problem, or thinking about and seeing the problem from a personal perspective. For example, a person who is 6-6 looks at a shelf on a wall and may not think twice about how they are going to get a glass down from that shelf, so they can pour a glass of water. A person who is 5-3 will look at that same shelf in a completely different way. "How thirsty am I? Do I want to put the effort into getting a chair or a ladder to get that glass down?" Significance helps us ask the question, "Why do I have my glasses so high on that shelf that I cannot get to them easily?"

My hope for Significant Recruiting is to show you how to ask the right questions:

1. Why do I want to play in college?
2. What am I willing to do to make that opportunity a reality?
3. How do I want to be perceived by those who may recruit me?
4. What are my ultimate goals once I get recruited?
5. What is the most practical and efficient path to accomplish those goals?

Over the past 10 years, I have served as a Head College Scout helping thousands of college coaches fill their rosters while evaluating and advising thousands of families with student-athletes who had the dream of playing in college. I have helped place over 4,000 of those student-athletes participating in 34 different sports and from every state in the United States and over a dozen countries worldwide at all five collegiate divisions:

- National Collegiate Athletic Association (NCAA Division I, II and III)

- National Association of Intercollegiate Athletics (NAIA)

- National Junior College Athletic Association (NJCAA or JC for short)

Most of those parents came to the first conversation with me with one of three objectives:

- My child wants to play in college

- My child wants to compete at the highest level

- We want them to get a full scholarship

They all had dreams of success for their child with no concept of the reality of what it would take from them and their children to plan, execute and achieve those aims.

My goal from the beginning was to create a simple but significant process for every family with a student-athlete who has collegiate dreams, so they could be able to learn, adapt and implement their college recruitment on their own. This was the genesis of <u>Significant Recruiting</u>.

I have worked with student-athletes whose parents were Fortune 500 CEOs, professional athletes and coaches, college and high school head and assistant coaches, athletic directors and principals, Hollywood movie stars, doctors, lawyers and engineers, university presidents, families with exceptional wealth, single parents, parents who were unemployed and even a few who were homeless, and every type of parent in-between.

What I have learned through all these conversations is that every parent, no matter their economic or educational reality, has 3 things in common:

- They love their child very much
- They want to give their child every advantage possible for their future
- They are at a loss as to how to get their child recruited by the right college coaches at the right colleges

Every parent is looking for an effective approach to help their child with their future. This playbook is designed to help you accomplish your goals without having to invest 10,000 hours, 10,000 dollars or 10,000 sleepless nights.

In the following pages, I have laid out a simple 12-step process that will not only put you in the best position possible to get recruited (success!) but will also help you (1) understand who you are, (2) what you need, and (3) how to be your authentic self—becoming significant along the way.

Before we move forward, though, let me share the number one reason I have for writing this book. My greatest passion for wanting to write this playbook is NOT due to my experiences as a coach, an administrator or scout. It comes from wanting the very best for my daughter, who has a dream of playing college volleyball.

Whether she actually plays is going to be fully up to her. What matters to me is that she has found something she loves and wants to pursue it. I cannot imagine a better outcome for my children than for them to find something they are passionate about in life and that inspires them to put in the work to make it a big part of their future. I would feel the same way had she said, "Dad, I want to be a graphic designer" or a professional dancer or a corporate lawyer or a heart surgeon. I am just happy she has found something she loves and is motivated and confident enough to really go for it.

What also got me excited about writing this playbook is that I now have the expertise that 30 years ago my parents, coaches and teachers did not have. My parents never went to college. My high school coach had no interest in helping me get to college and really had no idea how to help me get recruited even if he wanted to help. I had a big dream and no one knew how to guide me. In the end, I got lucky to have even worn a college jersey and to have competed in college, even though my parents and I made every mistake a family can make.

The information you will find in this playbook is the exact information I will be giving to my daughter. We will be following these steps with you!

I encourage you to read a chapter at a time, as a family, and be honest with each other. You may find that after Chapter 3, you are not ready for the recruitment process. You may have to go back to Chapter 1 and 2 and really dig in to make the ideas in those chapters stronger in your life before moving on to Chapter 4. The great thing about this playbook is that it will always be a guide you can count on to keep you on the right track. It is expected that at some point, you may have to take a step backwards, so when you are ready, you can take one significant step forward.

As you are going through the chapters, I am going to give your family real anecdotes and lessons from my experience as a coach and scout, so you can learn from the mistakes and achievements of those who have come before you. I will provide questions to ask, processes to follow, and perspectives from college coaches, former college and professional athletes and college administrators, along with websites to do additional research if you choose to.

My intention for this playbook is not to teach you a fancy new way to get recruited. It's to help you understand the best path forward, so each student-athlete can take ownership of their journey.

I am confident that your goals will be achieved if you commit to not just reading the 12 chapters but also putting in the significant but simple work that will be asked of you through each step. I encourage you to not just read it and attempt to memorize it, but also do your best to implement and relate each step to other parts of your life: relationships, faith, jobs, etc. Most of the steps will translate in a significant way to everything that is important to you.

As you read this book, know that I will be cheering for you! Let's go make your dream come true.

Chapter 1:
Commitment—Accept the Challenge

In the middle of every difficulty lies opportunity.

- Albert Einstein

I have spoken at dozens of high schools, camps, showcases, and tournaments all over the country. I have hosted and taught hundreds of recruiting webinars through the years. I have met one-on-one and face-to-face and advised more than 7,000 families. No matter who my audience is or where my audience is located, my first question to any individual or group of college prospects is always, "Are you committed to playing in college?"

Most student-athletes will nod their head or say, "I'm pretty committed." They are cautious because they don't want to give the wrong answer, or they don't want to show too much conviction to a stranger when they aren't quite sure where this question is headed. They often are afraid of telling the whole truth in front of their parents and then being forced to back it up later. There is also always a group of student-athletes who come out of their chair to confidently tell me how committed they are to being a college athlete.

I ask the question so I understand if this is going to be a 10-minute conversation or a 10-year journey. I don't want to waste the family's or my time, and the question "Are you committed to playing in college?" gets right to the point.

As the great Hall of Fame NBA coach Pat Riley once said, "There are only two options regarding commitment; you're either in or you're out."

It doesn't matter if we are talking about marriage, getting a job, flying to the moon, or writing a book, you simply can't do it part way and get the results you are expecting. You must fully commit to the time, energy, and attitude required to get to the end. Recruitment is a marathon. It is <u>not</u> a sprint. You must be patient. You must be humble. You must be open-minded to all the possibilities.

Commitment is the first step towards college recruitment because it is the key to everything, and it is not just the key for the student-athlete. Parents must make a commitment to this journey as well or the odds of their children playing in college go dramatically downhill very quickly.

When you are committed, you have pledged not only to become something or to get to a destination, but also to *do the necessary work* to become that something or reach that destination. Young athletes saying "I want to go to Stanford" or "I want to play at Division 1" are using dream or wish statements. They should instead be saying, "I need a plan to be the best student and athlete I can be" or "I am committed to doing the work in the classroom and in my sport to control my destiny."

It is important to understand the depth of what your commitment will look like and how it will be evaluated from the eyes of your high school coach and any college coaches who choose to recruit you.

Yes, commitment can look like getting up at 6am every day in the summer and running, lifting, and working on your skill set. A truly committed athlete may put in a full day's work before most teenagers roll out of bed to decide whether to go the mall or go to the swimming pool that afternoon. **Commitment is a pledge to do the uncomfortable.**

However, commitment is not just a student-athlete requirement for this journey. For a student-athlete to be committed, parents need to be just as committed. No, parents, you don't have to get up at 6am and run sprints with your child for them to become a great athlete. [It is great if you want to do that, but not necessary to their success.] That is your child's commitment, not yours.

Since this is a playbook to college recruitment to be shared by both parent and student-athlete, let's break commitment into two parts: Parent Commitment vs. Student-Athlete Commitment. It is important that both understand their roles and understand the keys to a significant recruitment journey.

Parent Commitment

Calendar: A parent's commitment starts with their calendar. Yes, you heard me right...*your calendar*. When your child's coach sends home the practice and game schedule at the beginning of the season and you agree that your student-athlete is committed to that team for that season, your student-athlete should be at *every* team event, practice and game…No excuses and no negotiations. Meaning: Do NOT schedule a 4:30pm dentist appointment on a day when you know your student-athlete has practice from 3-5pm!

Equipment: It is nearly impossible to become a college shortstop without a bat, a ball and a glove to use to practice. It is hopeless to try to become an all-conference point guard if you don't have a basketball to dribble at home. If money is an issue, go talk to your coach and Athletic Director. Give them a chance to find solutions to things you cannot afford. When in doubt, I love places like Goodwill, the Facebook Marketplace and Play It Again Sports, where you can find a good piece of used equipment for very cheap and sometimes even for FREE.

Emotional: Your emotional commitment as a parent starts with simply being present. You must be committed to paying attention to your student-athlete's mood and changes in attitude. It is important for student-athletes to hear your emotional commitment with words as much as actions. Make sure they hear things from you like:

- I love you
- I've got your back
- I'm proud of you
- Do you want to talk?
- Do you need help with anything?
- No matter what is going on in your life, I am here to go through it with you

Your child knows when you are manufacturing an emotion. They know when it isn't real. It is important for your student-athlete to hear conviction in your words and tone. Mean what you say. Say what you mean. Be you but commit to being emotionally present.

Time: There's a huge difference between *calendar* commitment and *time* commitment. Balancing parent-work obligations and athlete-team obligations can feel impossible at times, especially if you have multiple student-athletes in your home. Don't try and be a perfect parent, but make a commitment to three things every week, and you will be well ahead of the curve:

- Share Meals Together. No matter how good or how not-so-good your relationship is, your child needs to know that they can have you and count on you for a little bit each day.

- Attend Their Games/Events. Kids need to show you what they are doing and the results of the work they are putting in. They want so badly for you to be proud of them. When you make their events, they get the opportunity to give reason for your pride.

- Review Their Homework. It is amazing how many times I have asked a parent about their student-athlete's grades, and the parent said, "They are a good student... mostly As and Bs." Then I have them send me the student-athlete's transcripts and the student-athlete has a C average. Spending a little time each week to review their assignments and check on their grades gives your student-athlete a huge reminder that their grades are important because you are paying attention.

Experts: I became an above average basketball player because I watched Michael Jordan, Magic Johnson and Larry Bird play on TV as often as I could when I was a kid. I would take what I observed, and I would go outside and try to replicate it. I became a better shooter when my dad asked one of his friends who was a good high school coach to spend an hour with me working on my fundamentals. We don't always have to spend thousands of dollars for the top expert in the sport, but the more we can get our kids in front of people who really know their stuff and can teach what they know, the growth our student-athletes will see in their skills can be infinite. **You can't get better if you don't know how!**

Experiences: Take your student-athletes to see D2, D3, NAIA and Junior College athletic events. It breaks my heart when student-athletes say they are not going to pursue playing in college because they are not good enough for Division 1. There are 2,000-plus colleges and universities in the U.S. with sports programs and outstanding academics. You cannot go to a NCAA Division III (the lowest division athletically) game or event without seeing a student-athlete who was First Team All-Conference or All-State in high school. On top of that, 80% of all athletic scholarships are at non-NCAA Division I schools. Not choosing to follow your passion because you didn't get a D1 offer is like deciding to throw away your degree in Computer Science because you didn't get hired by Google. **The *opportunity* to continue to use your skills is much more important than *where* you get to use your skills.**

Communication: Poor communication, emotional communication or a complete lack of communication is typically where small issues become life-changing events. Remember, you have the ability to be positive, respectful, and humble. When talking to your student-athlete, make sure they know that you love them and support them through the good and the bad. Make sure they know that their coaches aren't perfect and are doing the best they can. Sometimes, we all just need to say, "I need some help" or "I'm not happy" or "Great job!" Saying "It was fun watching you play tonight" instead of "Why didn't you play more tonight?" can make all the difference between your student-athlete staying committed or quitting the sport altogether. College coaches are watching, listening, and asking questions about parents. There have been dozens of times when I stopped recruiting a student-athlete because of their parents and dozens of other times I should have asked more questions about the parents before recruiting a student-athlete. Remember, this is your student-athlete's present and future. When you don't have anything good to say, don't say anything until you can catch your breath and find a positive way to say what you are thinking and feeling.

Student-Athlete Commitment

Time: A student-athlete must commit to devoting time daily to working on their craft, athleticism and recruitment outreach. If the only effort you are putting into your craft is the two hours you put into your team's practice each day during the season, you are setting yourself up for failure. Less than 7% of all high school athletes will play in college.[2] What separates the 7% from

---

2   NCAA Research, "Estimated Probability of Competing in College Athletics," https://ncaaorg.s3.amazonaws.com/research/pro_beyond/2020RES_ProbabilityBeyondHSFiguresMethod.pdf

the 93% who will not play in college? **College athletes simply devote more time to getting better.**

Effort: Committing to going to the gym each day and committing to putting in the effort when you get to the gym are very different things. You feel the difference when you put in extra effort. You see your abilities improve. Your muscles are more sore. Your confidence is higher. Your coaches start paying more attention to you. If you are always:

- In the middle of the pack when coach has you run sprints or
- You are always the last one to practice or
- The first one to leave practice or
- You are the one who spends more time standing around in the weight room and less time lifting…

Then you are not putting in enough effort. **Work to be the first in everything you do.** That's a key attribute of the 7% who go on to compete in college.

Routine: The best leaders, students and athletes have one thing in common: they are creatures of habit. It is essential to commit to:

- Waking up at the same time each morning and making your bed
- Eating a healthy breakfast
- Getting your workout in
- Being consistent with when and where you study and do your homework
- Being consistent with the time you go to bed

The more regular you are with your life, the more those routines turn into significant progress.

Relationships: The most successful student-athletes are often the ones who have the strongest relationships with their teachers, coaches, parents and peers and are often the ones who are not afraid to ask for help:

- *Hey Coach, do you have time tomorrow to watch game film with me?*

- *Hey Ashley, do you want to stay after practice today to play a little one-on-one?*

- *Hey Mrs. Johnson, I'm struggling with today's chemistry lesson. Do you have time to review it with me this week? I really want to understand it.*

- *Hey Mom and Dad, I've been really down lately. I feel like I'm slipping in school and falling behind in everything I do. I don't think I can fix it on my own. Can we talk about what I'm dealing with and how to get back on track?*

Your commitment to relationships begins and ends with not being afraid to ask for help. The biggest mistakes I've made in my life were not building relationships with the people who were experts in my life. I had fantastic teachers in high school and college, and I didn't work to maintain those relationships. Teachers get into teaching because they love helping and working with students. You want to make a teacher's day, ask them if they have time to talk about the things you are struggling with. A good teacher will jump at the chance to help.

Nutrition: The old anecdote of **what you put into your body is what you will get out of your body** could not be more accurate. To be a great athlete, you must commit to putting healthy foods into your body. Young athletes burn calories at an exceptional level, even when they are just sitting around watching TV. Fruits, vegetables, water, and lean proteins are your best friends if you are an athlete. Make a commitment to making those four ingredients the centerpiece of what you eat, and your muscles will grow faster, and your endurance will increase dramatically. Stay away from soda, processed foods/sugar and dairy as much as you can as an athlete. They can often work against the improvements you are trying to make in your body's health, strength and energy. If you are not sure what you need in your diet, ask your doctor, a nutritionist or an athletic trainer. They are a great place to start.

Sleep: This is often the hardest commitment for teenagers. There is simply too much to see, do and experience in their young lives, so it is hard to let the body relax long enough to fall asleep at a decent hour. The key goes back to routine. I am a big believer in alarms. I have alarms on my phone and watch for everything including (1) when I wake, (2) when I take and pick up my kids from school, (3) when I have meetings, (4) when to workout, (5) when to go to bed, etc.

A teenager needs at least 9 hours of sleep each night to maximize their recovery and muscle, heart and brain capacity.[3] The best thing you can do to keep your sleep cycle consistent is to commit to reading or writing each night at a specific time. If you know you must be up by 7am, then you should commit to getting in bed around 9pm, so your mind and body can start

---

3   *John Hopkins Medicine, "Teenagers and Sleep: How Much Sleep Is Enough?" https://www.hopkinsmedicine.org/health/wellness-and-prevention/teenagers-and-sleep-how-much-sleep-is-enough*

slowing down to fall asleep around 10pm. Make sure to put the electronics away by 9pm. Turn off the phone, TV, tablets, etc. I'm a big fan of journaling for young athletes. They should always have a notebook or journal and writing tool by their bed. The more they put their thoughts on paper at night, the more they are moving their anxieties and stresses from their brains to that paper. If it's on paper, you don't have to worry about forgetting it. You have it written, so you can come back and deal with it later when your mind is ready to handle it. Your brain will thank you for it, and you will find that you will fall asleep faster without the worries of the next day on your mind.

Character: Last but far from least, I am going to lump the really important stuff that college coaches are looking for into one big category. When you think about committing to your character, I want you to think about the following:

- Values: Remember the golden rule—*Treat others as you would want to be treated.*

- Leadership: Be generous with your words, thoughts, abilities, fears, celebrations and compassion. Leaders share what they know, and people follow leaders because they understand that whatever they give to a good leader, they will get it back in multiples. **Be the role model you wish someone would be to you.**

- Coachability: You may not agree with everything your coach says. You might think there is a better way, but if your coach can count on every player to listen and get on the same path, suddenly you'll see growth, improvement, and consistency. Be the one who says "Yes,

Coach" and tries their best to implement what is being asked of you and the team.

- Teamwork: Whether you play an individual sport or a team sport, teamwork will always be the key to a successful season. Share, collaborate, discuss, challenge each other and expect those same things in return.

Husband & Wife College Coaches' Perspectives

Commitment and love will forever be intertwined. True love does not exist without commitment. So, when someone asks me why I was so committed to soccer from an early age, the answer seems obvious. As a kid I loved staying on the field after my game to see if anyone else needed players. I loved competing against players older, stronger, or the opposite gender than me. Playing the game was pure joy. As I aged it became obvious that soccer would be more than a recreational activity in my life. The training got harder and the stakes got higher. The love and joy of just playing evolved into the pursuit of challenges and achievement. It got harder, and harder, and harder as the levels progressed, which is why only a small percentage of high school players ever play in college. It's not often the skill level that determines which players continue. Skill level may determine what level a player achieves, but if the love of the game doesn't become a love for the challenge it will be hard to find success. Everyone loves the moment of achievement. You have to find a way to love the preparation it takes for that moment.

Lori Chalupny Lawson

- Head Women's Soccer Coach, Maryville University of St. Louis

- 2015 World Cup Champion

- 2008 Olympic Gold Medalist

- 2003 NCAA Division I National Champion

Airball. Airball. Those were my first two shots in a college practice. It wasn't from a lack of shooting ability. I had spent countless hours in a gym perfecting form and honing my accuracy. There were few people around who could outshoot me in an empty gym. But the addition of an intense and long college defender putting a hand in my face changed everything…and this was still only a drill. I thought I had a commitment to shooting but I was only committed to target practice.

While my playing career was limited, I found more success as an assistant coach for three different programs, most meaningfully Washington University in St. Louis, a high-academic NCAA Division III program in St. Louis, Mo. Commitment took on a whole new meaning in this incredible environment. Expectations to win Conference and National Championships were only exceeded by expectations of personal and professional success. On the bus to the game our guys would pour over the scouting report and study the film we had prepared for them to best understand their opponent. After the game? Whether a big win or heartbreaking loss you could expect to see textbooks and laptops open as they prepared for a different kind of test. Everyone has different advantages and disadvantages, but commitment is up for grabs. Commitment equals success. Not just because it is the clearest avenue to the success you're hoping for, but because the act of commitment is a life-changing win in and of itself.

Caleb Lawson

- NCAA D1 & D3 Assistant Coach
- 1 NCAA D3 National Championship
- 7 National Tournament Appearances

Chapter 1: Action Steps

- Talk as a family about the commitments above. Are you committed as a family to being the best version of yourselves?

- If your student-athlete has not demonstrated a commitment to certain things above, now is the time to set goals and expectations. Will they commit to doing their homework in the same location and at the same time each night? Will they commit to making their bed each morning? Will they commit to meeting with each of their teachers about working together to achieve a certain grade in each class? Put deadlines on accomplishing these goals.

- The student-athlete should schedule a time to meet with their coach, teachers, and guidance counselor to discuss a significant strategy to accomplish their goals. Ask for their advice and direction as well!

- Purchase or find a notebook/journal. Start creating a daily journal entry that includes the following:

o   Goals for the next day. Start small. Keep them simple.

o   Thoughts and feelings you have been dealing with that day.

o   Use it as a shared journal where mom/dad and student-athlete can write back and forth to each other… or even that your coach can reply or respond to!

Chapter 2:
Learn Your True Value and Reality

Face reality as it is, not as it was or as you wish it to be.

-Jack Welch

When Jake emailed me for the first time, he had watched a recruiting webinar I had hosted the night before, and he was writing to ask if I would help him with his recruitment. In his letter, he told me that he was from Vancouver, Canada, and that his dream was to play D1 basketball in the States. He gave me a few points of information about himself, but the one thing that caught my eye was that he was averaging 30 points per game for his high school team. He thought his scoring average would be the key to playing at the D1 level.

I called him that day, and we had a nice conversation. He was a good kid and hungry to be the best version of himself. I asked him several questions, including if he had any film of his team playing that he could send me. He told me that he went to a very small school and that no one filmed the games, but he would try and get me some film before his junior season was over. I gave him some tips on filming basketball games and what I wanted to see on film. He thanked me and told me I would be hearing from him soon.

A couple of weeks later, I received another email from him with game film. As a former NCAA Division III and Division II Head Basketball Coach for many years, it was rare for me to see kids who scored 20 points per game, so I was excited to see film of a kid who was putting up 30 points a night.

After watching the film, it was clear that Jake was legitimately scoring 30 points per game. He could shoot, dribble, and he had a strong understanding of the strategy and nuances of the game (high basketball IQ). However, within 30 seconds of watching his game film, I realized why he was scoring so much. There was not a player on the floor over 6-1 (most were under 5-8 including the forwards). Jake was maybe 5-11 ...maybe. Very few of the players on either team had any athleticism or special skills. It was obvious that Jake's coach didn't have much talent to work with and had built an offense for Jake to control the game as he pleased and shoot whenever and as often as he wanted.

At the peak of my career as a D3 (non-scholarship) Head Men's Basketball Coach, we had a Top 25 team in the country. We had a couple of kids who were talented enough to play scholarship basketball at the NAIA level and maybe the NCAA Division II level, but we didn't have anyone who had the size, speed or explosiveness to play at the NCAA Division I level. We had a solid group of kids who played extremely well together. It was their combined skills, talents and humility that made us great and led us to two Conference Championships and two NCAA National Tournaments in a three-year span. If I were to have recruited a kid like Jake during those years, he would have struggled to make our top 15 varsity squad as a freshman. His success as a high school player just wouldn't have translated to the college ranks. He had tremendous value for his small high school program, but his circumstances (i.e., lack of competition, lack of size and speed) were greatly affecting his ability to develop into a high-level college recruit.

When I called him after watching his game film, we had a difficult conversation about his reality, but he took all my constructive criticism in stride and with great humility. He asked what he could do to change his situation, and I gave him clear advice and direction based on his ability and goals.

He was a rare kid who put in the work and reached every goal I gave him. He took his natural talent and added hard work, smart decisions and a big dose of humility to get recruited. He ended up playing Junior College basketball for two years before transferring to a NCAA Division III school and having a very respectable college career.

Commitment and understanding your value and reality are the hardest parts of college recruiting for student-athletes and their parents. These are not easy to define concepts. For example, Recruit A might be 100 times more committed than Recruit B, but Recruit B might be a 100 times better recruit because of their size, speed and athleticism. Does that mean Recruit A should give up on their dream? Absolutely not! It just means that Recruit A might end up playing their sport at the D3 level and Recruit B *might* get the chance to play at the scholarship levels. They both have the chance to get a college degree, play the sport they love and potentially win a national championship, but embracing the reality of the game and their own skills and abilities is the key to this journey. If you really love your sport, does it matter what division level you get to play?

That is the reason I'm addressing value and reality early on—because it is important to understand that **your level of commitment may not determine your value, and your value may not be equal to your commitment.**

How then do you know your true value and reality?

Giving you black and white facts about value is an easy thing for me to do, but there are exceptions to every rule. Coaches are all different, and they see value differently.

I remember a D2 men's soccer coach who called me one day out of the blue and said, "Matt, don't send me recruits anymore unless they are at least 6'0" tall. We just got our hats handed to us by a team of giants and their size was too much for my little guys. I need to get bigger, and I only want to see big prospects from here on out."

About a month later that same coach called me back and said, "Matt, do you remember what I told you the last time we talked?" I said, "Yes, of course, Coach. You only wanted me to send you guys who are 6-0 or bigger. Haven't we been doing that?" He replied, "Yes, you have, thank you, but I want you to scrap everything I told you a month ago. We just lost to a team whose best player is 5-6 and he controlled the whole game with his speed and amazing touch on the ball. We couldn't stop him. I let my emotions get the best of me before. Please go back to sending me any kids at the positions we need who you think can play at our level. I want to see everyone no matter their size."

College coaches are finicky animals. They change their minds and get frustrated just like you and me. You can't control the ability you were born with, and you surely cannot control how a coach perceives you.

Let's focus on what we can control.

If you have heard me speak over the last 10 years, you probably heard me talk about the 3-Legged Stool. The three legs are Character, Academics, and Ability.

I chose this simple analogy because as a player, I always struggled with coaches who gave me too much information to learn and remember, and my anxiety would take over. I was and still am a visual learner, so the more I could see something first, the easier it was for me to learn; therefore, the birth of the 3-Legged Stool.

The 3-Legged Stool

The 3-Legged Stool is designed to keep the focus of a young athlete on the important things, but its greatest role is as a device that helps us understand our reality and value, as it pertains to getting recruited.

The 3-Legged Stool concept is extremely simple but tremendously effective when trying to motivate young people with the big dream of playing their sport in college. Kids often think that coaches are only focused on the things they can see:

- Size
- Speed
- Stats

What coaches really focus on to determine a prospect's value are the following:

1. Character (team fit)
2. Academics (university fit)
3. Ability (roster fit)

Imagine a leg falling off of a three-legged stool. What happens to the stool? That's right, it falls down. The same goes for a prospect's ability to get recruited. If there is a big deficiency in any one category of character, grades or ability, your recruitment may end before it begins. So put on your college coach hat and let's better understand how a college coach evaluates these three legs.

Character: Every coach in the country will tell you that the first thing they look for in a potential recruit is their character, but every coach defines character differently. I loved having a team full of diverse personalities. The more diverse we were, the sweeter the successes were because I knew we were doing something significant. We had brought a cast of characters together from all over the country who were introverted/extroverted, selfish/unselfish, confident/doubtful, energized/low-key and from different races, religions, political views and so on. If I could get all that diversity to work and play together and overcome their personal circumstances to buy into the values and mission of this new family they had joined, I knew our dedication to significance would lead to wins. In the end, it's a matter of how does a particular recruit's character fit the needs of our team.

These are just some of the questions a college coach will be asking about you:

- Is this student-athlete someone I want to coach for the next four years?

- Do I want to be around them for 80 practices, 25 games/meets, and 15 long bus or plane rides per year?

- Do I want to be around their parents before and after games and deal with them in-season and in the off-season for the next four years?

- Do they have a personality that fits our culture and/or adds a dynamic (i.e., leadership, sense of humor, easy-going, etc.) that fills in a missing piece for our team culture?

- Are they respectful, generous, compassionate, and collaborative?

- Will I have to worry about them in the classroom, the cafeteria, in the dorms, and when we are on the road at other colleges?

- Are they the type of person who will fall in line with the status quo, allowing us to maintain our strong culture, or will they shake up the status quo and challenge our weaknesses and therefore make our culture better? (I personally like a mix of both!)

- Do they treat the opposite sex with respect and equality? Do they represent their gender with dignity and humanity?

- Is this the type of young person who could become our team captain down the road?

- Do they have traits or experiences that give them the confidence to speak up and lead by example?

- Is this the type of person I would want coaching at our summer camps?

- Do they have the capacity to stay calm and clear-headed if they lose playing time or a starting job?

- How do they handle it when the going gets tough? Do they crumble when an official makes a bad call?

- Do they lose their head when another player says something disrespectful to them or if that competitor gets overly physical with them?

- Big-time D1 coaches will be asking this type of question: We play on national TV a lot and often play in arenas with 10,000-50,000 people in the stands. Do they get rattled by the pressure of a big audience with lots of eyes on them?

Look inside and ask these questions about yourself...and be honest. Would somebody watch you compete and answer these questions with positive responses? Would somebody overhear your parents talking in the stands and leave with a positive impression? Character matters. When coaches get fired, it usually isn't just because they didn't win enough games. Sometimes it is the coach's character. Other times it is the character (or lack thereof) of the players they bring into the university. In the end, character has an equal leg when evaluating talent.

Academics: To truly understand how college coaches perceive a student-athlete's grades and test scores, I like using the analogy of buying a car.

Let's say you are in the market for a new car. You've looked at your budget and know that you cannot afford to buy a new car at full price. You know that based on your income, you can afford to take out a loan from the dealership and pay no more than $300 per month for that new car. If you go over that $300 per month, you know you may not be able to pay your rent or your mortgage. You most definitely are not going to the BMW or Mercedes dealership because those brands would cost you $700 to $900 per month. You probably wouldn't waste your time with even a test drive. Why would you when you know you can't afford the payments?

A college coach uses the same mindset when recruiting a student-athlete because they also have a budget. A college coach understands that the average cost of tuition plus room and board in the U.S. is close $40,000/year[4]. Most families cannot afford to pay even half of that average price to attend one year of college.

A seasoned college coach will look at the academic standards of their university to determine the baseline of academic results they will require to even consider a student-athlete to recruit. They don't want to take the time to test-drive a recruit if they know they cannot even get that recruit through the application process. Why would they?

Another thing to keep in mind is that the better your grades, the more scholarship and financial aid you will receive from a college/university. The more scholarship and financial aid you get, the more likely a college coach will know they can make their school affordable for you and your family.

---

4   U.S. News, *"See the Average College Tuition in 2022-2023,"* *https://www.usnews. com/education/best-colleges/paying-for-college/articles/paying-for-college-infographic*

I have received hundreds of phone calls from college coaches over the years asking me to help them with their recruitment needs. The first point of emphasis is always grades. Poor grades and test scores to a college coach is like a dark alley in the middle of the night. They aren't going to go down that path if they don't have to. The reality is that there are enough kids with good grades that these coaches don't ever need to go down that path for the ones who don't.

Ability: Your typical college coach will evaluate well over 100 recruits each year to fill each open position they have on their roster. So, if a coach is graduating three seniors, they are going to evaluate close to 300 recruits to fill those three roster spots.

To properly evaluate 300 recruits' abilities, coaches will start evaluating those kids at the beginning of their freshmen year in high school or sooner. Before those 300 recruits reach their junior year, the coaching staff will attempt to do the following to properly assess each of those 300 recruits in terms of ability:

- Watch multiple game films
- Watch each recruit play live
- Invite them to a camp to work with them individually

During this process, the coaching staff will be consistently ranking and re-ranking their list of recruits, often adding and subtracting recruits from the list while placing "the keepers" into three tiers: (1) Immediate impact recruits, (2) Potential impact recruits, (3) Developmental recruits.

An ***immediate impact recruit*** has the ability to make a significant impact to the team immediately.

A *potential impact recruit* has the ability to make the team and help the program in the long-term and maybe the short-term.

A *developmental recruit* has a special quality about them, but are lacking strength or balance or fundamentals. For example, there are not a lot of 7-0 tall basketball players walking around, so a coach may take a chance on a kid of that size knowing they can coach the strength, speed and skill into the frame.

Most coaches will attempt to get the list of 300 down to a list of 10 recruits for each position of need by the time they officially make an offer. Once they have their list completed and tiers ranked, they will do the following:

- Make phone calls and begin doing deep research on their Top 30

- Set up unofficial visits (family pays for the travel to campus) with their Top 10

- Set up home and official visits (college pays for the family's travel expenses) with their Top 5

Once their research and visit process is complete, and they have a strong assessment of each recruit, they will typically re-rank their tiers by position and are now ready to make offers. They will then make an offer to their #1 recruit for each position. If that recruit turns them down, they will move on to their #2 recruit and so on. In the end, strong programs are going to evaluate your talent and ability over a long stretch of time. If you are a coach with full-ride scholarships, you must take that $40,000-$60,000 investment into one recruit very seriously. You are typically not going to make that type of offer to a kid by only seeing one film or without the opportunity to see them compete live.

You may be asking yourself: *Can't you be a really good recruit with amazing talent but have poor grades and still get recruited?* Of course you can, but as you sit there as a family talking about your child's future, are you really saying, "Hey, don't worry about your grades, just be a great player" or "Isn't your dream to go to a tiny school in the middle of nowhere where they don't care about your character and grades because you can hit a tennis ball at 100 mph?" No, I didn't think so. You are talking about going to Stanford and Michigan and Alabama. Those coaches can get any kid they want. Do you really think they are going to take a kid who only has one or two of the three legs?

3 Legs or Nothing

My two young assistants walked into my office many years ago excited about a big kid they had just seen on film. They enthusiastically encouraged me to go watch this 6-8 stud play live at his high school. They told me that the kid was from a tiny town, and no one was recruiting him. When I asked about grades, they nearly came out of their shoes to tell me that he was an honors student with solid test scores. They were very clear to tell me that not only could we get him into school, but we could also probably get most of his tuition paid for with an academic scholarship.

It was right before the holidays, and we had a rare couple of nights off from practices and games with our players at home, so I got in my car that following afternoon and drove the four hours to watch this kid play. I got to the gym early and was able to watch some of the junior varsity (JV) team play before the varsity. As a college coach, I never wasted a chance to watch younger players play to maybe catch lightning in a bottle and find one to two other future recruits in the gym I might like.

The JV game ended, and soon after, the two varsity teams ran out on to the floor to do their pre-game warm-ups in a layup line. The young man I was there to watch immediately grabbed my attention. There was not another kid on the floor for either team bigger than 6-3, so I knew immediately who my target was.

When this big, young man got the ball for his first lay-up attempt, he lackadaisically strolled in and just threw the ball up without even looking at the rim and missed the basket by about a foot. He slowly lumbered back to the end of the next line without a care in the world. He did take the time to joke with some of his classmates in the stands.

I was not thrilled with my first impression, but I brushed it off knowing there was a long night ahead of me for this young man to prove his worth. On his second trip through the lay-up line, he did it again. No effort. No leadership. No commitment to being a role model. This time his teammates all raised their hands to give him a high five when he walked by to go to the end of the line, and he faked the high five and jogged by laughing at his big joke. At this point, my instincts made me look over to the other side of the court to see if his coach was paying attention to what I was seeing. Sure enough, I could tell the coach was agitated. When the young man got back to the side where his coach was, I could tell that the coach was not happy and was letting the young man know how he was feeling about the kid's lack of effort.

What the coach knew that the young man did not, was that a college head coach was in the stands to watch him play that night. I always called the high school coach before making a visit to get their permission to visit their gym and to give them a head's up that I may want to talk to him and his player after the game. This coach knew I was there. He was excited someone was coming to watch his player. I asked him (like I always did) not to tell the young man I was coming to the game. I like to see recruits in their natural environment playing for their coach and team...and not for me.

After the coach gave this young man a bit of a chewing, the young man lifted his arm and brushed the coach off as if to say, "Oh Coach, you are overreacting...it's just a warm-up."

Although I just drove four hours on one of my rare nights off to watch this kid play, I had seen enough. I got up and I walked out of the gym and drove the four hours back home. I didn't even stick around to see the jump ball to start the game. The next day I told my staff to take the young man off our board.

They fought me on him. They said "Coach, he is the kid we've been looking for. He's got size and a skill set that will make him the best player in the conference by his sophomore year. We've got to have him."

I looked both in the eyes and told them, "If I recruit that kid and bring him to our program, we will all be out of job by his sophomore year because he will be the cancer that tears our team apart." Yes, this young man had two exceptional legs of the 3-Legged Stool, but the third leg—character—was such a deficiency that he could no longer be an option for us.

The reason kids fail in getting recruited is not that they don't understand the principles of the 3-Legged Stool. The problem is that most parents and athletes do not really understand their child's reality. Like the young man in the above story, he simply thought being tall and having good grades would be enough. He was failing to ask the right questions: (1) How good am I? (2) How am I being perceived? (3) Am I doing enough to separate myself from my competition?

I recommend four paths that a student-athlete can take to get clear answers to these questions:

1. ***Play your sport in the off-season*** with a club or travel team. College coaches typically coach their teams at the same time you are playing your high school season. When you play for a club and travel team, it is much easier for college coaches to see you perform and provide a proper evaluation of your skill-set when they get to see you do it live as a member of an organized team.

2. ***Send your game or skills video*** (we will talk about how to do this the right way in Chapter 5) to a few college coaches at each division level and ask them directly to evaluate your ability to play at their division level and their school.

3. ***Attend the camp of the colleges/universities you are interested in attending.*** I recommend attending camps at each division level when possible. It is important to get an unbiased assessment from coaches at all levels. Don't just go and see what happens. On the first day of camp, approach the Camp Director or the Head College Coach

running the camp, and ask them if they would find time while you were there to watch you play and then provide you with feedback on not only your ability level, but also what you need to be working on to get better.

4. *Schedule a one-on-one evaluation with a recruiting service*. You will have to provide them with game or skill video ahead of time but ask them to provide their verbal or written evaluation of what they see on film and what their perception is of your character and demeanor, as well.

A Former NCAA D1 Player and Father's Perspective

As a former Division I athlete, I often find myself reflecting on the "what ifs" of my own decision to pursue the D1 path over a lower level of college basketball. While my collegiate experience was undoubtedly rewarding and shaped me in many ways, I've come to realize the importance of thoroughly considering all options before making a final decision. While I was trying to find the court at the University of Wyoming on a full ride, my younger brother was having all kinds of success at the D3 level. My oldest brother was my biggest basketball influence and hero as a small college NAIA All-American.

In our journey through my son's recruiting process, Coach Rogers guided us and constantly engaged in dialogue about the various levels of collegiate athletics. We knew that weighing the pros and cons of each opportunity would be essential in finding the best fit. It was a process that required us to think critically, seek guidance from mentors, and evaluate our son's long-term goals. The allure of

Division I scholarships was not there for us, which made it easier to seek alignment between my son's aspirations, abilities, academics and the opportunities offered.

While witnessing my own child navigate the recruiting process, I encouraged him to explore every option available. I understood that every athlete's path is unique, and what may be the right fit for one person may not be for another. Together, we analyzed factors such as academics, team dynamics, coaching philosophies, and future career prospects. By thoroughly considering all options, my son was truly empowered to make an informed decision that would shape his college experience both athletically and academically.

Quinn Wirth

- Former NCAA Division I Basketball Player
- Member of the 1986-87 University of Wyoming Sweet 16 Team

Chapter 2: Action Steps

1. Student-athletes: Schedule a meeting over the next month with each of your Head Coaches and your teachers. Ask them if they would write you a detailed assessment of your character, coachability/teachability, and skills/grades. It may be a few sentences or a paragraph or a couple of pages. It is so important that you know how your teachers/coaches perceive you, so you know the reality of your relationship but also what their true expectations are of you.

2. Get a professional evaluation. I encourage you to investigate the following types of professional evaluations:

   a. Play on a club or travel team in your high school off-season, so college coaches can watch you perform live more often.

   b. Send film directly to college coaches at each division level asking for their assessment.

   c. Attend camps or combines at colleges you are interested in at each division level.

   d. Schedule a recruiting service evaluation or assessment.

Chapter 3:
Own Your Academics

When I first met Thomas and his family, I disqualified him as a potential college basketball prospect in my mind within minutes. He was at the end of his junior year, and neither Thomas nor his parents could answer my basic questions about his grades, test scores, work ethic, relationships with coaches and teammates, stats, etc. Every answer was vague and only elicited more questions and red flags.

There seemed to be a great divide between Thomas and his parents regarding his ability and goals, and I especially did not like the lack of respect he used when talking to his parents. His parents struggled to answer how committed he was and how committed they were to supporting him in this venture, and that irritated Thomas, and he let them know that in a way that I didn't appreciate.

When I asked about his cumulative GPA, they hemmed and hawed and said they thought it was a "2-something." They did mention that he had had an F or two and a few Ds, which greatly concerned me. It made me think that there was a real chance that the "2-something" GPA could be lower than they were letting on. I made sure they understood that he would not be able play at the NCAA DI level without at least a 2.3; the NCAA D2 or NAIA level without at least a 2.2; and although there are no set GPA standards for D3, it is nearly impossible to get a D3 coach to recruit you without a 3.0. Though there are D3 schools that can admit students at the same academic minimums of D1, D2, and NAIA, I let the family know that they wouldn't get very much scholarship or financial aid, if any at all, with Thomas's present grades. Depending on his actual GPA, Junior College could be his only option.

It is never good when a family cannot answer the basic questions every coach in the country will ask of them, but it always worries me the most when one parent is especially silent, and Thomas's dad had barely grunted two words since we started to talk. So, I asked the dad what he thought about his son's desire to play college basketball, and his one-sentence answer was enough for me. The dad quickly helped me clarify what my next steps should be when he said, "He just doesn't work hard enough as a high schooler, so I don't know why we are even talking about college or college basketball."

It was clear that dad was not on board and was frustrated we were even having a conversation about something so far-fetched, so I moved forward with some critical questions to find out how I could challenge this young man before I would even consider working with him. I also wanted to see if I could at least get the parents and myself unified. I wanted Thomas to know that his mom, dad and Coach Rogers were all on the same page.

"Thomas, if I walked into your bedroom right now, what would I see?" I asked.

Both of his parents laughed out loud at the question. Thomas hesitated at their laughter and quietly said "It's a little messy." His mom quickly followed that statement with a huff and said, "It looks like a tornado went through his room."

"Thomas, where do you do your homework every night?" I asked next.

He paused and said "I don't have one place. It kinda depends on my mood." Again, his mom and dad chuckled in response to his reply and to Thomas's obvious dismay.

"Thomas, how committed are you to playing college basketball?"

"I'm 100% committed. I want to play college basketball more than anything else." That answer elicited nothing but silence from his parents.

"Your mom and dad don't seem so sure about that," I said. "You don't know your GPA. You can't articulate what your relationship is with your coach and teammates. You don't seem to have consistent study habits or any direction as to how you are going to accomplish your goals, and you don't take pride in how you take care of your things. Can you see how those are some big concerns for your parents and me?"

Then his confident voice finally came out.

"I do have direction," he said. "I have started my own company. I have built a website, and I am already making money from it. I love playing basketball, and I want to go to college and get a degree to continue to grow my business."

Both parents finally spoke up with some pride in their voice.

"He has worked very hard to build this and make money," his mom said.

"It's the one thing that he's ever started and stuck to besides basketball," his dad added.

Confidence with sincerity! I finally heard what I was hoping for. This was a kid who just didn't fit into a traditional school setting, but he was motivated and obviously passionate. He was able to learn (I knew I wouldn't even know where to start to build my own website or make money from it), and it was clear to me that he needed a different approach than the typical kid I worked with, so I initiated a course of action for him to test his ability and dedication.

"I very much appreciate your talent, and I'm impressed that you have built something from scratch that you are proud of, but those things are not enough to even begin considering putting a plan together to help get you recruited or even attempt to introduce you to college coaches, so I am going to challenge your passion you are telling me you have and give you some goals. If you can accomplish these goals, then we will have a follow-up conversation and decide if we want to move forward together with this journey. Are you open to that?" I asked.

Thomas responded that he was willing to do anything to get the opportunity.

I said, "Okay, if you're ready, write these things down."

I gave him six specific goals that had to be accomplished, including sending me his official transcripts, before I would consider working with him. He finished writing down my requests.

"If you can complete all these steps in the next six weeks, I want you to call me with the changes you have made and the impact those changes have made in your life. Now, when I say I want **YOU** to call me, I mean exactly that. I won't move forward to help you if mom or dad are the ones who call me, or I just get a vague email from you. This is your journey. You need to be accountable as the master of this journey. Are you willing to accept my terms?"

"Yes, coach."

"Mom and Dad, are we in agreement on these terms?"

"We like what we hear, but we still have our doubts that it will be more than words from him. Let's see if he will follow through," his dad said.

As we hung up the phone, I had zero expectations that I would ever hear from this family again. I felt somewhat content that I had saved this family a lot of money they would have spent hiring me to help a son who didn't have his act together, and I hopefully made a dent in this young man's psyche and maybe got the wheels turning that it was on him to change his personal direction, and maybe just maybe our conversation had motivated him enough to begin improving his relationship with his parents, teachers and basketball family. Sometimes, that is all I can hope for.

Then six weeks later it happened. I'm rarely shocked anymore after all these years of working with kids and families, but I will admit that I was surprised. Thomas called me. Not his mom. Not his dad. Just Thomas. He said, "Hey Coach, it's Thomas. I wanted you to know that I just emailed my transcripts to you. I've worked through all the goals you gave me, and I am calling to set up a follow-up conversation with you, me and my parents."

I couldn't tell if I was dumbfounded by what I just heard or proud. I did my best to respond without complete surprise in my voice.

"Thomas, that's great news. I am very proud of you for following through, and I'd be happy to meet with your family again."

When we got back on the phone together a few nights later, it felt like I was talking to a completely different family than the one I spoke to six weeks earlier. They were present, coherent, focused and seemingly motivated.

There was an honest disappointment in the parents' voices when they shared that they had not been aware of how poorly Thomas was actually doing in school, but they also seemed proud of the work he had done since we last talked.

"I'm really proud of Thomas for putting the work in that we have discussed; however, I did look at the transcripts he sent me, and he doesn't have the 2-something GPA you thought he had when we last talked," I told them. "He went into the spring semester of his junior year with a 1.8 GPA, which pretty much eliminates any possibility of him getting admitted to a four-year college. What came from your conversations with your teachers and guidance counselor?"

Thomas was quick to respond, "My guidance counselor said that school policy allows me to replace two grades, but I must re-take those classes. I can take one this summer and take the other this fall. If I can get Bs or better in those two classes that I failed before, I can improve my GPA from a 1.8 to a 2.3. I have also worked with all my teachers in each subject, and I am on track to have a 3.0 for this semester, which also will improve my overall GPA."

"That's great news, Thomas! How does it feel to know that you asked for help, and your teachers responded accordingly?" I asked.

"Surprised, I guess. I convinced myself that my teachers didn't like me, so I didn't like them. Most of my teachers seemed happy that I was asking for help, and I wanted to do better in their classes. I don't know why I was so afraid to ask for help before," he shared.

"That makes me very happy for you. That was one of my biggest regrets from high school and college. I simply didn't work hard enough on building relationships with my teachers and professors, and I realize now how much that hurt my progress. I'm glad you have figured that out faster than I did!"

Thomas ended up getting his GPA to a 2.5 by graduation, had about 15 college coaches talk to him after we started working together. He ended up playing for a small D3, graduated and today continues to grow the business he started back in high school.

Although Thomas's story may not resonate with many of you who already have a strict academic structure and are diligent with your study habits, I hope what does resonate with you is the power of consistent communication between parents and student-athletes, as well as consistent communication with the school and teachers. The student-athlete being in control of that communication is key and can have a positive effect in improving the overall experience they have with their teachers. I have made academics and Thomas's story an essential part of the <u>Significant Recruiting</u> program because most families don't understand the impact grades and relationships play in the recruiting process.

College coaches will call your child's teachers, guidance counselors and coaches. They won't just ask about the GPA. They will ask about your child's efforts, communication ability, class participation, collaboration with other students and how those educators feel about the child's and the parents' character.

As a college coach, there may not be any part of my academic assessment of a student-athlete and their parents that is more important than knowing if you are a family who works to create positive outcomes together and supports a positive learning environment. Are you willing to learn? Are you willing to adapt/compromise? Are you capable of building and maintaining relationships? Are you willing to ask for help and accept coaching? Can you follow instructions and execute expectations and goals?

Over the past few years, I have worked with several executives to help them hire the best people for their organizations. It is extremely rewarding for me as a lifelong teacher and coach to hear CEOs and hiring managers talk about how much seeing collegiate athletic experience on a candidate's resume means to them and the advantages that experience provides their organization. Those executives talk about the qualities they crave that are often found in candidates with an athletic/team-oriented background: direct communication, the ability to build quick rapport with colleagues and clients, resilience to overcome obstacles and failures, and a desire to collaborate and work as a team for the betterment of the whole instead of just focusing on personal success.

Gallup, on behalf of the NCAA, did a study in 2020 surveying 74,385 U.S. adults with at least a bachelor's degree. It found that "college graduates who participated in NCAA athletics enjoy a host of positive long-term life outcomes at greater rates than non-athletes, among them well-being."

Another remarkable thing about the study—especially in light of the growth Thomas made just by opening his mind to improving communication with his parents and teachers—is that former "NCAA student-athletes strongly agree their professors cared about them as a person (35%) compared to non-athletes (28%). NCAA student-athletes are also more likely (27%) than non-athletes (23%) to strongly agree they had a mentor in college who encouraged them to pursue their goals and dreams. And they are slightly more likely (67%) to strongly agree they had at least one professor who made them excited about learning than their peers who did not participate in NCAA athletics (65%)."[5]

Hopefully, I have motivated you a little with this chapter, but at the very least, you should be excited about the significant impact college athletics/academics can have on your recruitment in the long term.

---

5   Gallup, Inc., "Gallup-NCAA: Student-Athletes Thrive in Life After Graduation," https://www.prnewswire.com/news-releases/gallup-ncaa-student-athletes-thrive-in-life-after-graduation-301082384.html (published June 24, 2020)

A College Coach's Perspective

The process of recruiting is an exciting time for high school athletes. Their athletic skills have drawn the attention of college recruiters who will make a pitch for their talents. The student-athlete is looking for the right fit, both athletically and academically, that will give them the greatest chance of success at the next level. Although academics are never ignored, all too often the athletic opportunities receive the greatest attention of the prospective athlete.

Their conversation with the college is often through a coach, who may or may not present a balanced picture of what to expect as a college student athlete in their program. The coach can give the prospect a good overview of the academics, but the real picture is painted by the various academic departments and majors. One must look deeper to understand what to expect from the academic experience and how it can contribute to the student-athlete's future. It is important to remember that the primary mission of every school is to educate. The athletic experience contributes to the education, but does not define it.

Every incoming student, whether an athlete or not, must be prepared to make a commitment to the academic component of the school. If they don't, they will not receive the educational benefit of college and most likely will not have a good experience. I have always encouraged prospective student-athletes to look for the right academic fit before looking at the athletic fit. Regardless of their academic skill set, there is a school that will fit their needs as long as they are willing to make the academic commitment.

One time during my tenure as the men's basketball coach at Washington University in St. Louis, I had a father bring his son to my office to talk about the basketball opportunities we could offer him. I had not had any previous communication with the son, and he was not on my recruiting radar. He had researched the academics of the school and was intrigued by the strong pre-medical program. By his own initiative he submitted an application and was admitted in the spring of his senior year. They were now going to look at the basketball programs at the schools where he was admitted. I was surprised when I recognized the father as a former NBA champion and a current successful NBA coach. The son was a talented athlete with many college opportunities, but his father wouldn't let the athletic component override the academic component. The son enrolled at Washington University and became an All-Conference player on a very successful team. More importantly he graduated and was accepted into medical school. Today he is a successful doctor. Success at the college level is attainable in a variety of ways. Recognizing this during the recruiting process will give the student-athlete the best chance of maximizing the value of their education.

Mark Edwards

- 685 Wins in 37 seasons at Washington University
- 2008 and 2009 NCAA Division III National Champions
- Three Final Fours (2007, 2008, 2009)
- 21 NCAA Appearances
- 15 Conference Championships
- Three-time National Coach of the Year (2002, 2008, 2009)
- 30 All-Americans, including 2008 National Player of the Year

Chapter 3: Action Steps

- Meet with your guidance counselor to evaluate your present academic situation and develop a plan to graduate with a specific GPA.

- Schedule an ACT or SAT exam by the end of your sophomore year. Plan on re-taking that exam at least one to two more times.

- Schedule a meeting with each of your teachers at the beginning of every semester to discuss:

  o Goals

  o Behavioral expectations

  o Study habits

  o Extra credit and tutoring

Chapter 4:
Create A Personal Game Plan

The biggest risk is not taking any risk...
In a world that is changing really quickly,
the only strategy that is guaranteed to fail is not taking risks.

- Mark Zuckerberg

I've been asked hundreds of times by parents, "At what age should we start our child's recruitment?" The answer is always the same. "You start when your child tells you they are ready to start."

Sometimes that happens when the student-athlete is 13 years old, and sometimes it doesn't happen until their senior year of high school. No matter the age a student-athlete says they are ready and committed to the journey, you start when the student-athlete is determined to move in that direction, but that doesn't mean you should wait to start planning for college or the potential of playing in college.

I've heard way too many families say that they were told that college coaches either don't or can't start recruiting until after a student-athlete's junior year begins. That advice could not be further from the truth, and is often the reason outstanding prospects don't get recruited or end up having to settle for colleges that are below their ability level or simply do not fit their needs as a college student.

College coaches can start evaluating athletes any time they want. Yes, there are many rules that college coaches must follow regarding when they can make contact with a recruit and when they can offer or sign a recruit, but they can start evaluating any time. College coaches may be looking at a student-athlete well before a student-athlete decides they want to pursue competing in college. That is why it is so important for a student-athlete to be in control of their process early.

Don't give control of your recruitment to anyone!

Typically, where I see families lose their way in the recruiting process is when they transfer the control of their child's recruitment to someone else. Have you ever heard a parent say something like this:

"Our club coach told us that they have a high-level recruitment program, and they bring in lots of college coaches to their practices, so we are confident our daughter will be seen by college coaches."

Or

"Our high school coach told us that college coaches really don't get serious until a recruit's senior year, and he said he would make phone calls to college coaches at that time if our son still wants to play in college."

When I hear these types of comments from parents, it breaks my heart.

Imagine you want to buy a house, and you hire a realtor to help you through the process, and your realtor says, "I'm going to take great care of you, and we are going to have you moving into the house of your dreams in no time."

The problem with that pseudo-confident statement is that your new realtor has not asked you any of the following questions first:

- Do you want to live in the city, suburbs or in the country?
- Do you want a previous lived-in home, or do you want to build a new home?
- Do you want to be near any schools or near your work or near other family?
- How much square footage are you looking for?
- How many bedrooms and bathrooms do you want?
- How many children and adults will be living in the house?

When a club or high school coach tells you they are going to take care of your recruitment, and they don't ask you some of the following questions first, it should raise a lot of red flags:

- How far away from home do you want to go?
- What do you want to study in college?
- What size of school are you looking to attend?
- Do you want to go to school in a big city or in a smaller community?

- How important is it to you to be able to play right away as a freshman?

- Do you want to play at a school with a proven reputation of success or are you comfortable going somewhere and building your own legacy of success?

When coaches do not ask these questions, they are forgetting that you are the client, and you have needs and wants and priorities. Recruitment is a two-way street. Yes, we want coaches to recruit you, but we also need to remember how important it is first that you want the school and the school can provide you what you desire for your future.

I never agree to work with a family until I have asked the above questions and many more. I never make any promises to a family until I know what they want, and what they need, and until I am confident that I can help them achieve their *realistic* hopes and dreams.

Why Start Early?

Most families have a very hard time thinking about college and recruiting before their student-athlete is at least 16 years old. Many parents cannot fathom why a college coach would want to recruit someone who has so many years of development ahead of them. I often ask families the following question to help them better understand why the early bird gets the worm:

Think of the last big vacation you went on where you were going to be gone more than a day's drive from your home for a week or more. How much time did you put into deciding:

- Where you want to go

- What your budget was for the trip
- How you were going to get there (i.e., plane, bus, rental car)
- Where you were going to stay

My wife and I took our kids on a trip to Disney World and then a Disney Cruise several years ago. My wife started planning that trip well over a year before we left. She did her research on location, travel, reviews, costs, etc. Because we are careful with our money, we bought our plane tickets and booked our hotels many, many months before the trip, when the prices were at the lowest. We took advantage of every piece of advice we found on-line about how to have the best experience and save the most amount of money. We talked with other families who had done a similar trip before we did. We were only going to be gone for seven days, and we took 12 months to plan it.

The college decision is a life-altering decision that will last at least four years and affect the next 50 years. Do you really want to start thinking about that type of decision during your senior year of high school?

Below are the top reasons why starting your planning early is so important:

Coaches Have Already Started

- College coaches start recruiting student-athletes in the 7th and 8th grades.
- 80% of Division I recruits will be found by the end of their sophomore year of high school.

- The competition is fierce. There are over eight million high school athletes in the U.S. alone. Less than 8% will make a college roster. Less than 1% will play Division I.

- If college coaches do not know who you are, you are not on their recruiting board. If you are not on their recruiting board, they are recruiting other athletes instead of you!

Recruitment Doesn't Start When a Coach Contacts You

- No matter the NCAA or NAIA rule, college coaches can watch a recruit play on film or on-line any time. They will attend practices, showcases, and camps to evaluate potential recruits before being able to contact those recruits.

- Most college coaches will take anywhere from one to two years to evaluate a recruit before making an offer and sometimes before they ever make contact with a recruit. A recruit could be on a coach's radar today without them even knowing it.

- The sooner college coaches know who you are, the sooner they can begin evaluating you, even if they cannot communicate with you yet.

Early Process = Better Decisions

- By starting your recruitment as early as possible, you are putting yourself in the driver's seat.

- You want to always start your recruitment (when possible) while coaches still have plenty of roster openings and scholarships are plentiful.

Questions to Ask As a Family

- Do we want the opportunity to visit and compare multiple college campuses?

- Do we want the opportunity to speak with and compare multiple college coaches?

- Do we want to be able to learn how our student-athlete is perceived and valued at every division level?

- Do we want the opportunity to maximize our scholarship and offers?

- Do we want the opportunity to be able to choose the school that fits our student-athlete the best academically, geographically, financially, socially and athletically?

If the answer to all those questions is an emphatic "YES!" then you are beginning to understand why starting early is so important.

Now that you understand the importance of starting early, it is imperative that we put a game plan together that is individualized and personal.

What are your priorities?

Below are the questions I recommend you ask as a family. It is important to not limit yourself to just the ones I have listed. Think about you and your wants and needs. I promise you will think of other questions that are just as important to your future. It is also important to write your questions down on a sheet of paper, a notebook or a spreadsheet and write/type out your answers. We will use those questions and answers later in Chapter 12.

- How far from home are you willing to go? If the coach at UCLA or Duke or Wisconsin or Texas called tomorrow and offered you a full scholarship to come play for them, would you be comfortable going to that part of the country or that distance from home?

- Is there a specific climate you want to live in? Sunny and warm 365 days per year? Somewhere with a full four seasons? Maybe you are a baseball player or golfer—is being able to play outdoors 12 months out of the year important to you? What do you think you would love doing for a career for the rest of your life? (The wrong question is "What do I want to major in? ") Regardless of playing your sport, remember that you are going to college so you can earn a degree to do something with your life that will satisfy your soul and give you a happy life. Not every school has an Engineering or Marine Biology or Nursing or Architecture program. If your dream is to be an architect, how much time do you want to put in to talking to college coaches who coach at a school without an architecture program?

- What size of school would you be comfortable attending? Are you the type of kid who could handle being at a school with 40,000 students, living in a 25-storey residence hall that houses 1,000 students or taking a class with 300 other kids? Or would you feel more comfortable on a campus that only has 1,200 students and where the average student-teacher ratio is 15-1? Do you see yourself as a little fish in a huge sea or a big fish in a small pond? Don't just think about your sport. Think about how you make friends. Think about how you like to eat your meals. Think about how far you want to walk every day to get to your classes.

- What type of coach do you need? Do you want a coach who is loud and passionate and has no fear of yelling and challenging their athletes? Do you prefer a more emotionally conservative coach who is more fun-loving and allows their athletes to find their own motivation?

- What culture and demographics are you looking for in a school? Does diversity matter to you? Is the ability to join a fraternity and sorority important to you? What are your social, political and religious views? Do you want to be surrounded by people with similar belief systems or do you want to go somewhere that is more tolerant and open-minded to all thoughts and beliefs and life-styles? Too many kids do not put enough thought into this part of game-planning, and those are the kids who end up calling me a year or two later wanting to transfer because they put too much weight into playing time and how much they liked their coach, and they did not put enough time into asking questions about fit.

- What positions are you open to playing in college or what events are you open to competing in at the college level? You might be the star quarterback on your high school football team, but a college coach may see you as a Running Back or Wide Receiver at the college level. Are you open to changing positions or competing in different events?

Questions for Parents to Ask of Themselves

Is Junior College or Prep School an option for our student-athlete?

a. Is two years playing at a Junior College (JC) or Prep School going to help our family with the short-term and long-term costs?

b. Does our student-athlete need a couple of years at a JC to not only save money, but also to get bigger, stronger, faster and/or more mature?

c. Would two years at a JC help increase our student-athlete's value with a scholarship school that perhaps they do not have today?

d. How far away from home are we comfortable with our student-athlete being?

e. What type of coach do we want them to have?

f. Is the reputation or academic prestige of the school important to our decision?

IMPORTANT: One of the questions I don't want you to discuss too much right now is "What is our budget or what type of school can we afford?" I have seen too many kids and families put up major roadblocks in their decision-making process because they look at a school's full costs and get scared away. They simply cross a school off their list because they can't imagine paying that $50,000 price tag. It's important to note the Federal Government gives out over $234.6 billion in aid each year and 85% of all college students receive some level of financial aid or scholarship.[6] Remember, these schools are not immune to the needs of the average family. All universities understand that very few families will ever pay the full price tag or could even consider half of that price tag. The key is to go through the evaluation process with every school that fits you and has interest in you. You won't know what the out-of-pocket costs are going to be until the very end of this journey. The best advice I can give you is to avoid considering a school's price tag until you know there is a mutual interest between you and the coach, and you understand what they can do for you financially.

I could go on and on with questions you should be asking at the beginning of your game plan, but it is important that you start asking questions that are significant to you. Not only should you be asking these questions before anything else, but you should be prioritizing which answers are more important than others.

Monthly Action Goals

Find 10 minutes per month to review and complete the following:

1. Keep making your grades and test scores your priority to improve each semester (Chapter 3)

2. Build an on-line recruitment profile and update that profile at least once per month (Chapter 5)

3. Choose at least 50 to 100 colleges (five to 10 per month) you want to invite to recruit you (Chapter 6)

---

6   CollegeBoard, "Trends in Student Aid: Highlights" (2022), https://research.collegeboard.org/trends/student-aid/highlights#How%20Much%20Aid%20Are%20Students%20getting?

4. Email your on-line profile and interest to at least four to five new college coaches per month (Chapter 7)

I encourage you to write this out or type it out and print it. Put it on your bedroom mirror or on the fridge in the kitchen or put a monthly calendar alarm on your phone to make sure you are accomplishing these goals. Persistence is the key from here on out.

We still have a lot of work to do, and we must accept that this is a marathon and not a sprint, so patience continues to be very important. However, we are well on our way, and these monthly action goals should start to become an enjoyable routine. There's a good chance that this is the first and last time you will ever get recruited for anything. It should be enjoyable. You are going to have coaches who want you to be a part of their team! There's nothing better than being wanted and appreciated. Don't forget that as we keep going.

A College Coach's Perspective

When deciding on a college, specifically small private colleges, like the one I coach at, I always advise families to consider the part of the country the student-athlete may want to live in after they graduate. As an example, our university is located in Southern California. If Southern California is an area that they want to live in after graduation, then they should seriously consider looking at schools in that region. I want them to think about alumni networking, internships, jobs, and the lifestyle they want after graduation as much as I want them to think about me as a coach and the quality of our education. In the end, I want kids who want to stick around for four years and maybe find a long-term home in our area.

Chris Krich

Head Football Coach, University of La Verne

- 12-Year Veteran Head College Coach
- Conference Coach of the Year
- 1 NCAA National Tournament

Chapter 4: Action Steps

- Have a notebook or spreadsheet where you save your answers to the following questions and any that your family adds:
  - o What distance from home are you willing to go?
  - o What geographic locations do you prefer?
  - o What do you want to do for a living and study in college?
  - o What sizes of schools are you open to attending?
  - o What type of culture and diversity do you prefer?
  - o What style of coach do you prefer?
  - o What positions or events are you willing to play or compete in at the college level?
- Refer to the chart in Chapter 12, which will help you organize your answers to make good decisions at the end of your journey.
- Complete your monthly action goals.

Chapter 5:
Build Your On-line Resume

If you're waiting until you feel talented enough
to make it, you'll never make it.

- Criss Jami

To begin this chapter, I want you to put your college coach hat on. I want you to imagine you oversee your own college program. The University President has put you in charge of building a program with integrity that embraces a balance of sport, academics, community service, strong values and character...and one that will consistently be in the Top 4 of the conference year in and year out. You are now responsible for the following:

- Hiring, supervising and developing a coaching staff

- Managing an annual operations budget

- Fundraising the thousands of dollars needed to run a college program that needs to compete above and beyond what is given in the operations budget

- Building a culture of support from the student body, faculty/staff and community at-large, so there are fans in the stands

- Growing a culture of pride and financial support from the program's alumni community

- Ordering your program's equipment and uniforms and maintaining your facilities (gyms/fields/pools, weight room, locker rooms, etc.)

- Scheduling a full complement of home and away contests/games/events with other colleges and universities

- Finding, evaluating and recruiting a full roster of student-athletes who are academically acceptable to the school's admissions standards

- Finding scholarship and financial aid for all these student-athletes

- Convincing the parents of these student-athletes to send their child to play for you over the dozens of other coaches potentially recruiting them

- Keeping those kids healthy, happy, going to class and staying out of trouble

- Building a culture of inclusion, teamwork, tolerance, hard work, commitment, goal-sharing and WIN-NING...don't forget winning!

You have a $20,000 operating budget. That is all you have for the entire season to pay for EVERYTHING, and you must play in 25 contests. You are going to have 15 student-athletes on your roster. You have two assistants, a graduate assistant and a team manager. You have the following needs that will quickly drain that $20,000:

- Uniforms
- Travel gear
- Practice gear
- Coaches gear
- Equipment (i.e., balls, nets, sticks, bats, helmets, etc.)
- Transportation to 12-14 away contests
- Meals for 20 student-athletes, coaches and staff who will be traveling to each of those away games
- Housing for any overnight trips (Remember: If you have a male coach/manager for a female team or a female coach/manager for a male team, they must have their own room)

Did I mention that the University President has made it clear that he/she wants you competing in the National Tournament in the next three years if you'd like to keep your job?

Okay, so look at the needs list above. What's missing from our expected costs?

You guessed it: RECRUITING.

If you are running a half decent program, you are not making your team stay at rat-infested hotels, or expecting them to wear cheap uniforms that won't last the season or use poor quality equipment. You also know how important it is to make sure your players are eating right, so you are not taking them to greasy fast food restaurants for each meal, so that $20,000 is probably all gone before you even think about getting on the road to start recruiting the student-athletes you need to have a team to coach.

So, what do you do with no budget to recruit?

Well, 20 to 50 years ago, you built relationships with every high school coach within a 100-mile radius of your college. You called them on the phone and said something like this.

"Coach Johnson, I hope you are well. This is Coach Rogers down at Teacher College, and I wanted to see if you have a Power Forward (or Third Basemen or Outside Hitter or 200 Meter Sprinter, etc.) in your senior class who you think could play for me?"

Now, don't get me wrong, those relationships are still being built today and those conversations are still happening. The problem is that your President wants you in the National Tournament in the next three years and to have a winning program every year, and there simply isn't enough talent in that 100-mile geographic radius to accomplish those goals. The teams in your conference are recruiting the best talent coast-to-coast and even internationally. *College coaches are recruiting and making offers to kids as early as the 6th grade.* You are going to struggle to just recruit seniors, and you can't just recruit in your area if your program is outside of a huge metropolitan area like New York City, Chicago, Los Angeles or Houston. There are different challenges in large city areas, as well. There are often eight to 10 other colleges and universities that are all trying to recruit the same talent in those cities, in addition to the D1 coaches with million-dollar budgets who can fly into your region and easily poach kids by offering bigger scholarships, budgets, national attention and NIL (Name, Image, Likeness) money to them.

Also, it's April, and you just got the job, so all the best talent for the upcoming season has already been recruited and has committed to their college of choice...even the NCAA Transfer Portal has been thinned out, so there just isn't much left to make an immediate impact on your program unless you want to take a chance on kids with behavioral issues or questionable histories. Your President also told you he/she wants you to focus on integrity and character, so you don't want to take a lot of chances on kids who could end up hurting you more than helping you (see the 3-Legged Stool in Chapter 2). So, you are not going to bring in a lot of program-changing talent in that first year. That leaves you with no recruiting dollars and maybe one full year to build a national contender. No problem, right?

So, what do you do if you are the Head Coach? How do you pull a rabbit out of an empty hat?

Deep breath. Exhale.

Remember, it's not 20 to 50 years ago. We have the World Wide Web now, and the internet has everything including access to the best prospects on the planet...right at your fingertips... right from the phone in your hand.

Most college recruiting will begin on-line. For the same reason you go on-line to shop before going to the store, college coaches need to be efficient with their time and money.

The key is understanding that most college programs do not have the budget to travel out of state or even out of their extended geographical area to recruit more than a few times per year. Not even the Big 5 Conference coaches have the time or the man power to get everywhere and see every kid compete.

Your job as a family is to make sure every coach in the country can sit in their office and find you. There is no better way to do this than to have your child's athletic and academic profile on-line on a website that every college coach in the country utilizes to recruit. Whether you create a profile at NCSA, Sports Recruits, Captain U, etc., is not as important as what you do with it. Please hear me loud and clear when I say that I am never going to recommend that a family pays for one of the services offered through one of these companies, but to not take advantage of at least their free services is, in my mind, a huge mistake. With most of the on-line services, you can create a free account and profile. Your child's profile is immediately visible in their database for college coaches to search and find.

Let's use a scholarship baseball coach as our example. That coach is sitting in his office and knows he is graduating seven seniors next year. He has zero recruiting dollars. He needs seven incoming freshmen or transfers who can all come in and contribute right away.

His program is in Kansas, so he doesn't have a huge metropolitan area close by where he has tons of local talent to choose from, so he focuses his geographical search on kids in Kansas and the surrounding states of Oklahoma, Colorado, Nebraska, Iowa, Missouri and Arkansas, where he knows a lot of kids go unnoticed. He also knows that he and his staff can drive to most of those locations in a day when they need to go watch kids play live or do a home visit.

This coach does have some athletic scholarship dollars, but the most he could probably give one recruit is $5,000 to $10,000 above and beyond their academic scholarship and financial aid the school will give them.

He logs into his coach portal through one of the above on-line services, and he begins to input his search requirements. He wants kids who have an on-line profile that includes film, stats, game schedule, contact information, grades and test scores, so he can get an idea of their ability and recruit-ability.

He knows that to get a recruit through the door at his school, they must have at least a 3.0+ GPA and a 21 ACT. This coach knows that his school costs $40,000/year and with those specific grades and test scores, the school will give a student-athlete about $20,000 in financial aid and academic scholarship, leaving the family paying about $20,000 out of pocket each year.

With that in mind, the coach focuses his search on kids with a 3.5+ GPA and 25+ ACT. He understands that families do not make decisions based on just being admitted. He knows that families make their final commitment based on what the family can afford. He understands that by recruiting kids with grades and test scores well above his university's admissions standards, those kids will get much bigger academic scholarships; and therefore, he will not have to use as much of his athletic scholarship budget to get them admitted. Because he is saving athletic scholarship dollars by recruiting kids with higher grades, he can now spread his scholarship dollars around to more recruits and get more talent on his roster.

With his search criteria now entered, he clicks "Search" and within seconds, he has a list of 30 names on his screen, including every junior baseball player in those states that fit his criteria. He now has 30 potential recruits who have created a profile with a personal statement that allows the coach to get a good idea of their character, grades and ability immediately. What the coach really loves is that he has not had to spend a dollar out of his pocket or his program budget to find these kids. He loves that in minutes he can watch their film, verify their grades and call their high school coach or even pick up the phone and call potential recruits directly.

Now, let's say you are a junior baseball player in Nebraska. You made Varsity as a freshman. You were First Team All-Conference as a sophomore. You just led your team to the Final Four in the State as a junior while serving as the team's Captain. You have a 3.8 GPA and a 28 ACT. However, you do NOT have an on-line profile. The above coach will contact all 30 of the recruits that popped up on his search in the next few days. You will NOT get a call because you do not have an on-line profile. With your grades and test scores, ability, character and program fit, the above coach would have been able to give you a full academic + athletic scholarship if he only knew you existed.

The recurring message of this playbook will be: If college coaches do not know you exist, they are not going to recruit you. I do not know one college coach in the country in any sport who doesn't use on-line recruiting services to make their process simpler and more efficient.

College coaches are crazy competitive and often great innovators. They love finding something that works that their competition doesn't know about. You will rarely hear a coach boast about how they are recruiting or how they are winning. They will almost always keep that information close to the vest, but all college coaches use on-line platforms to find, evaluate and communicate with recruits even when they publicly say the opposite.

A College Coach's Perspective

On-line resumes have been very helpful in our recruiting process here at the University of Hawaii at Hilo (NCAA Division II). While going to school, playing basketball, and experiencing Hawaii's culture and Aloha spirit makes for a memorable student-athlete experience, it can be challenging to recruit here. Distance of travel, cost, and time make it difficult to do in-person evaluations on the west coast (or anywhere on the mainland United States). Even watching in-state recruits can be difficult because it still requires an airline flight. I usually make one recruiting trip to the mainland a year and will try to do some in-person evaluations while traveling for games with our team during the season. But catching a game on one of our road trips can be difficult because of the challenge of the recruit's schedule fitting with our schedule.

When we have access to on-line resumes that we can filter to meet the requirements for our school and program, it is extremely helpful. We can identify countless numbers of recruits that we would never have known about if it weren't for their on-line resumes. As a result, we are able to start with a much larger, and often higher quality, pool of recruits. The resumes are also helpful later in our process as we start to research and try to determine which student-athletes are a good fit for our program. Having access to a highlight or game film, transcripts, contact information, and a personal statement gives us a good snapshot of the recruit and saves a lot of precious time.

Dave Kaneshiro

Head Women's Basketball Coach, University of Hawaii at Hilo

- 23 Years as a Head College Coach
- 3x Conference Coach of the Year

Chapter 5: Action Steps

- Research the best recruiting services available with the most college coach usage

- Schedule phone assessments with two to three of these services

- Build a free on-line profile with at least one of these services

- Update your profile at least once per month

Chapter 6:
Construct a Diverse Attack List

Who you are tomorrow begins with what you do today.

- Tim Fargo

I'm feeling generous, so I am going to give the student-athlete reading this my credit card (metaphorically, of course). I am going to drop them off at the mall of their choice, and I am going to tell them that they have $5,000 to spend however they want.

I pick them up at the mall three hours later, and they hop in my car with what they have purchased.

Which recruit is you?

Recruit A: In their bag is one item. Maybe it is a $5,000 watch. It is the watch every 17-year-old dreams of. It's the type of watch where you walk around with your arm up in the air, so everyone sees it wherever you go. It's so beautiful, you can imagine it sitting in a glass box at the Louvre in Paris next to the Mona Lisa.

Recruit B: There are so many bags, we barely have room to fit them in the trunk and the back seat of the car. This recruit bought an iPad and iPhone, a new laptop, Air Pods, a full new wardrobe of clothes, 10 new pairs of shoes, some hats, a few belts, some bags, and some new sports equipment.

Both recruits get into my car feeling like huge winners. They thank me a thousand times over and can't believe their luck.

Guess which recruit will find the most joy and the least regret with their purchases?

If you said Recruit B, you are correct.

The biggest mistake any recruit makes is that they put all their eggs in one basket. They focus on one or two colleges or one Division or one Conference and won't consider any others. There's nothing wrong with wanting what you want, but a lot of kids don't consider the risk that comes with those decisions and choices.

What if you find out at the start of your senior year (when it's too late to change plans) that the coaches at those two schools you have focused on have decided not to make an offer to you?

What if after applying to both of those schools in your senior year, you don't get admitted to either school?

What if both coaches at these two schools do recruit you? You get accepted to both schools, but you must pay $40,000/year, and your family can't even begin to consider paying that amount of money each year.

What if you get an offer at the end of your sophomore year of high school, and you verbally commit to a full-ride scholarship to attend your dream school? A year and half passes. You are midway through your senior year, and you get a phone call that the coach has decided to retire. The school has hired a new coach who is rescinding the scholarship offer that the retiring coach offered to you.

You looked at one school. You had zero communication with other coaches. Well, you did receive lots of voice mails and emails from other coaches at other schools, but you never took the time to call or write back. Now that you are desperate, you try and call all those coaches back. They are now the ones not returning your calls. The coaches that do respond, politely say, "I am sorry, our class is full. If you would have only responded to us 18 months ago, we may have been able to help you. Good luck. We hope you find a place to play."

That beautiful watch you bought on your spending spree got stolen last weekend at a club tournament when you couldn't help but show it off to everyone. When the watch was stolen from your bag during the tournament, you realized you had nothing to show from your shopping spree because you made a spontaneous and impractical purchase. Regret.

I hope you feel the disappointment and stress and regret in your mind and body that these decisions have caused you. I want it to hurt now in this hypothetical world we are discussing. I want it to hurt badly. Why? Because if it hurts now in this fantasy world I have presented, I can only hope that I can keep you from making these same types of mistakes in the real world.

Now, imagine you were the recruit who had kept their options open. Your number one choice might have fallen through, but you've maintained relationships with option B, C, D, E, F and G. You may still be disappointed that your first option fell through, but you have great options to fall back on.

Likewise, imagine how you would feel if you were the one who bought 50 items with your shopping spree. Yes, you went to school with your new pair of shiny white shoes, but you failed to look at the weather that morning to know that it was going to rain all afternoon. After school you got your new shoes soaking wet and accidentally stepped in a mud hole and completely ruined the shoes. It's sad, but guess what, you have nine more new pairs sitting in your closet at home that someone else paid for. There's still some regret, but you can get over it a lot faster. Can't you? Hopefully you have also learned your lesson to pay more attention to the weather before you go outside with the other nine pairs of shoes you have left. No regrets.

Now that we've learned how to shop the right way, let's explore how creating a diverse Attack List of schools you want to pursue can lead to the most success. A lot of recruits can still put themselves in terrible situations, and that will make me very sad if they do, so I'm also going to share some ground rules for approaching your attack list before you start picking schools.

Creating an Attack List

1. Start with 50 to 100 schools that fit the answers to the questions you asked in Chapter 4.

2. From there, make sure to narrow down your list to at least 10 schools at each NCAA D1, NCAA D2, NCAA D3, NAIA and JC level.

But Coach Rogers, I only want to go to big schools, and I really only want to play at the D1 level.

I want to live in a $5 million mansion and drive a Ferrari. Just because I want it, doesn't mean I am going to get it. We must be realistic at this point. Your reality may be that you are a true D1 athlete and already have D1 coaches sending you information, and those coaches may have already reached out to your high school or club coach expressing their desire to recruit you. These are all fabulous things, but don't forget about the regret you felt above. Now is not the time to divert from the plan. Now is the time to hope for the best but prepare for the worst.

For those parents who are still skeptical about making your child look at college divisions their child simply does not want to attend, it is important that we start talking about the L word. That's right, LEVERAGE!

How to Leverage Your Attack List

When we talk about creating a school list or attack list, it is essential that we understand how big of a role leverage plays in our final results. Again, I will bring you into the mind of a college coach and begin getting you comfortable with how coaches will actively recruit you. The following scenario should help a lot.

Scenario 1: First College Coach Phone Call (recruit is unprepared)

The phone rings on a Tuesday night, and it is the Head Coach at Big State University. Your family just finished dinner, so mom and dad are there to listen to the conversation. The

Head Coach says they are calling to let you know that they received your email with your on-line profile, watched your film, looked at your grades, and they think you have the potential to be a great fit for their university and program. You are excited because your efforts are already creating results and with one of the top schools on your attack list. You sent the invitation, and you have a coach already responding.

Three minutes into the conversation, the coach at Big State asks you a question.

"Do you have any other schools recruiting you?"

You were not prepared for that question, but you quickly respond with, "No Coach. You are the first to call me!"

You think this will make the coach feel great because this means that the coach can put all their energy into recruiting you, and you can put all your energy into getting excited about Big State University. You quickly put the phone on mute and whisper to your parents, "We did it. Coach Rogers was right. It worked! I can't wait to tell my friends I am going to Big State University."

You are right about one thing. The coach at Big State U was excited to hear that they were the first and only coach to call you so far, but not for the reasons you think.

On the other end of the line, the Head Coach at Big State U is quietly doing a little fist bump. They love the fact that they can now take their time to recruit you and figure out if they really want you on their roster. They don't have to offer you a visit yet. They don't have to talk scholarship dollars with you yet. The coach can play the long game with you while continuing to recruit other players while hopefully finding someone better than you. The coach holds all the cards and has all the leverage. The coach is the only coach recruiting you, so you have no other options but Big State U, at the moment.

Then the coach responds to you.

"Well, that's great! Keep your head up. You are a really good player, and I am sure this is going to be the first of many calls you are going to get. I'd like to keep an eye on you throughout the summer. Would it be okay if my staff and I call you every once in a while to check in on you and see how your club season is going?"

You are obviously deflated by this response, but you keep your composure and say, "That would be great, Coach. I am so thankful you called. Feel free to call any time."

The coach has heard everything they hoped they would hear and unceremoniously ends the conversation with, "You will hear from us for sure. Keep working on getting stronger and quicker. I am excited to watch your new film when you have it. I will look forward to our next conversation. Say hello to your parents for me and have a great summer! Goodbye."

As the phone call ends, you turn to your parents and say, "What? The coach said they really liked my film, didn't they? Didn't they say that I was what they were looking for? No talk of an offer or scholarship or commitment? Check in 'every once in a while'? What does that mean?"

Remember what I have been preaching since the beginning of the playbook. These coaches are looking at sometimes hundreds of potential recruits and consistently evaluating their process and fit for their program.

This was simply the initial call to gain some essential information about you:

A. Is this a good kid? Do I like them?

B. Can this kid hold a conversation?

C. Do they have good energy?

D. Are they polite and respectful?

E. Is there confidence in their voice?

F. How involved are the parents? Is the kid leading this process or is there a parent driving it?

G. Are any other coaches recruiting this kid?

It is imperative that you build your Attack List with the purpose of creating leverage. The more prepared you are for any scenario, the more that leverage will make a difference in who makes you an offer and when and how. Let's reimagine the above phone call with you knowing you have leverage in your pocket.

Scenario 2: First College Coach Phone Call (recruit is prepared)

The same introductory phone call from the Head Coach at Big State U happens in this scenario. This time you understand before that first phone call that you need to keep your emotions and expectations in check, but still show great energy and respect to the coach. Be prepared with a list of questions that you can ask any coach when they call.

When the coach this time asks, "Do you have any other schools recruiting you?" you are ready to rock.

"Thank you for asking, Coach," you reply. "I've just started the process of reaching out to coaches in the past couple of weeks, and I have sent my information to about 50 colleges, but Big State U is one of my focus schools. I have had about 20 of those coaches look at my on-line profile and several coaches have already emailed me back with their interest in me. It's early, but I am excited to have conversations with any college coach who is interested in me helping their program. Do you have time to answer a few questions?"

Now, the coach is the one who is a little taken aback. They are not used to calling recruits who have their act together. You have already impressed the coach with your character and preparation in the first minute of them calling...YOU! The coach knows this kid is in control of their destiny.

"That is great news! You have your act together and that makes me very happy for you. I am not surprised. After watching your film and reviewing your academics, I knew I was going to have my hands full getting you to play for me, but I am in for the long haul. You've already got me sitting up and paying attention, and I hope I can convince you to let me go through this journey with you. Ask away. I'll do my best to answer all your questions."

You are completely empowered now and understand that the leverage is now in your hands. You begin asking your prepared questions:

1. *What do you like about what you see on my film and how do you see me fitting into your roster as a freshman?*

2. *Are you graduating any seniors at my position? Would I have a chance to compete for a starting job as a freshman?*

3. *How many recruits are you planning on signing in my class?*

4. *Do you have a time line in place on when you will be making offers and hope to finish my graduation class?*

5. *With my grades and test scores, can you give me an idea of what our family's out-of-pocket costs might look like at Big State U?*

6. *Do you have any scholarships left, and do you see me as someone with the potential to earn a scholarship in year one?*

7. *Do you have any advice or recommendations for me about my recruitment or how to improve my skills?*

And just like that, you have made the absolute most out of this initial conversation with a coach. Here's what you've been able to create:

- The coach is impressed with your confidence and preparation.

- You have a solid evaluation about why the coach called you in the first place and where the coach sees you fitting on their roster.

- You know what the competition is going to look like for playing time and the chances of you getting to play right away if you ultimately choose this school.

- You have a much better idea of what the out-of-pocket costs are going to look like and the reality of a potential scholarship.

- The coach gave some great advice about how to move forward to help your recruitment.

You turned a devasting result from the first scenario into a confidence-building, information-gathering success in the second. Just by creating an attack list with many diverse options, you are putting yourself in the driver's seat. Coaches cannot take their time to recruit you or just put you on a list for consideration. They must take you and your timeline seriously, or they know they can lose you to another coach and program at any point.

It's a Learning Process

As you go through the process of creating your attack list, remember what you learned in this second scenario. Even if you are only focused on big schools or small schools or schools in a certain region of the country, it is essential that you are always gathering information about fit and value to help you with your endgame decision-making.

There are a variety of things that you want to learn as you go through this process, and building a diverse attack list will help you accomplish all the below goals:

1. *Interview Experience:* It doesn't matter if it is a major D1 coach or a small D3 coach at a school you have never heard of. Every opportunity you receive to interview, ask questions, build rapport and find confidence on the phone and in front of coaches is pure gold.

2. *Understanding Value:* A D1, D2 and D3 coach might call you and tell you that they think you are talented and a good fit their program. The D1 coach might be open to redshirting you (having you sit for a year as a practice player before beginning your four years of college eligibility) in your first year, but never makes that possibility

clear. The D2 coach might be open to you playing on their Junior Varsity team (yes, colleges can have JV programs) for a year if they find you aren't ready. The D3 coach might be bringing in 10 to 12 recruits, and they may not know what that final number will be until May or June of your senior year—two to three months before you move to campus. The more you listen and ask questions to coaches at each level, the more you are going to know the difference between the dream and the reality.

3. ***Setting Priorities:*** I can't tell you how many times a family has told me that their priorities going into the recruiting process are (1) free education, (2) playing time, (3) close to home, (4) a great coach, (5) a winning program, (6) a family culture, (7) Ivy League/world-class education—then halfway through the recruiting process, they realize that their top priority really is #5 or #6 on their list. Be open to your needs and priorities changing much more than you expect.

4. ***Gaining a Sense of Self-Worth:*** No matter what happens in the end, you want to walk away from this process knowing that you can handle any situation you end up in. You need to know that no one can take your value away from you. It is yours to give and no one's to take. If you are determined to put the work into building relationships, being coachable and being a great learner in and out of the classroom, then you will do exceptionally well wherever you go because you will be focused on making the most of all situations.

In the end, this is a learning process. Instilling a healthy and positive sense of self-worth in kids is my #1 goal for any kid I coach, train or mentor. It should be every family's goal to go through this process knowing that the "dream" school may not end up making an offer or being a good fit. Creating a robust attack list and the leverage that comes with it makes the disappointment of potentially not getting recruited by the "dream" school much more palatable because of all the wonderful options you have created and get to choose from in the end. Keep that in mind the next time you go on a shopping spree!

A College Coach's Perspective

It makes no sense to close off any option as a prospective student athlete. Never has it been more competitive to just make a college roster. With the transfer portal enabling transfer athletes to immediately be eligible to play for their new school, the recruiting game has completely changed. Teams are getting older instead of younger, and I do not expect this trend to change any time soon. This means coaches can be more, and are becoming more, selective with the high school athletes they choose to accept. Having coached at all three levels (NCAA DI, II, III), now more than ever I am looking for a way to eliminate a prospective student athlete. The prospects who do not show active interest or engagement and who are not prepared are easy to spot and eliminate. Now more than ever parents and prospective student-athletes have information at their fingertips. There is no excuse to not have prepared for each encounter with a college coach. Every opportunity is a chance to impress and earn a spot on a college roster. Student-athletes who are prepared and take hold of the process will without a doubt rise to the top of college coaches' recruiting lists.

Rich Reed

Head Men's Basketball Coach, University of La Verne

- Co-Chair of the National Association of Basketball Coaches Committee on Academics
- 14 Years as a Head College Coach
- 5 Years as a NCAA D1 Assistant

Chapter 6: Action Steps

- Create an Attack List of at least 10 schools at every division level. Aim for 50 to 100 schools on your Attack List at minimum.

- Type up a list of questions you want to ask college coaches when they call you or when you call them. I recommend using the Notes section on your smart phone to keep this list. You never know when you are going to be talking to a college coach, and it is smart to have your questions a click away.

Chapter 7:
Send the Invitation

*Each new day is an invitation
to an adventure of your own making.*

- Steven Redhead

Several years ago, a father asked me how many college coaches I directly knew. I told him that I couldn't even begin to guess. With 25 years as a high school and college coach, athletic director and scout, I have met and befriended a lot of coaches and built a lot of relationships. However, this dad wouldn't accept that for an answer, and he asked, "How many college coaches could you find on your phone and call right now?" I told him, "Fine, I will take a few minutes and count my contacts for you." By the time I got through surfing through my entire contact list on my phone, I counted 97 college coaches in my contacts with personal cell numbers. He was surprised by my answer and said, "Wow. That's a lot, and more than I expected."

The reason we were even having such a conversation was because they were one of the families who was upset that their high school and club coaches weren't doing more for their son's recruitment, and they were determined to make the high school coach the fall guy for the reason no one was recruiting their son.

I asked them why they thought their coach would (1) know how to help them with their son's recruitment, and (2) have college coach contacts to help them? They really did not know how to answer either question, but I explained that they were assuming that since their high school coach was a basketball coach that he must have access to all the college coaches and understand how they recruit and what they needed on their respective rosters.

That frustrated the dad, and that is why he immediately challenged me with the question about my contacts and ability to communicate with college coaches. He needed me to provide a level of credibility that was satisfactory to him.

I told him that the average high school coach (1) didn't play in college, (2) may have played in college but never coached at the college level, (3) did coach at the college level, but had been out of college coaching long enough that they no longer had the contacts they used to have.

I asked him a few questions to help him understand how hard college recruitment is for high school coaches:

Does your coach have a full-time job teaching at the school? Yes.

How many players in the full program? Four teams of 12, so 48.

Does he have a family? Yes. He's married and has three kids of his own.

Did he play in college? Yes. He told us that he played at a junior college for two years, but that he didn't move on to a four-year program because of a knee injury.

Did he ever coach at the college level? Yes. He said he was a D3 assistant his first year out of college, but that was 20 years ago.

So, what you just described to me was someone who hasn't played, coached or recruited at the college level in 20 years, and he hardly had any experience recruiting except for one year at a non-scholarship program. He is now a high school coach who teaches all day and goes home at night to take care of his family while finding time to grade papers and prepare the next day's lesson plans, and you expect him to take care of the recruiting strategy of 48 young men when he probably has zero college contacts and no idea what any college coach needs on their roster next year. Your coach is in the exact same position you are in. For him to help you, he would have to search college athletic directories and cold-call college coaches hoping they will answer or return his phone call. Does that about sum it up?

Silence.

I recently had a great conversation with one of the top NCAA D2 women's basketball head coaches in the country. She carries a roster of 15 players each year, she typically graduates three to four seniors each season and we were discussing the recruiting class she just finished up to replace the four seniors who were about to graduate.

I asked her how she found this year's four recruits that had already committed and just recently signed their National Letter of Intent (NLI).

She paused, and it was clear that she was trying to remember the process she went through with all four of her new recruits, and then she laughed and said, "They found us. Well, I take that back. Three of the four contacted us and expressed their interest in our program. The fourth has been coming to our summer camps since she was in middle school, and we've had a great relationship with her and her parents for years. She actually committed to us when she was a high school sophomore."

When I asked if that was an unusual class because all their signees reached out to them first, she didn't have to put too much thought into her response.

"Not really. Look, I don't want to come off as over-confident, but [our college] provides a world-class education, and our program is consistently ranked in the Top 20 in the country. Last year was the first time in my nine years here that we didn't go to the National Tournament." I could hear the smile on her face as she said, "We will fix that next year."

"Lots of recruits email and call us every year. That doesn't mean we make an offer to every kid who asks us to look at them, but we work hard, if we have time, to evaluate their film and watch them play live if they do contact us. This class happens to include two all-state players from out of state. So, we may never have known about these two great kids if they didn't reach out to us and express their interest."

As a good friend taught me many years ago, *the invitation is the key to everything.*

I am going to talk directly to the parents reading this chapter for a bit. Let's think about your personal history.

How did your first date come about? Did somebody ask you out or vice versa?

If you are married, which of you mustered the courage to propose to the other?

Think about all the jobs you've had over the years. Did you ask an employer if they were hiring, or did you send them your resume and express your interest in joining their organization?

I don't know when the concept got lost as it pertains to college recruitment, but the biggest misconception I hear from families is that it is somehow taboo to contact a college coach.

I don't want to burden the coaches. If my son is good enough, they'll just find him, right?

If I've heard that excuse once, I've heard it a hundred times.

If you really think about it, isn't that a ridiculous thought? We've somehow turned high school coaches into professional recruiters/admissions counselors and turned college coaches into these omniscient god-like figures who are all-knowing and all-seeing and are too good to pick up the phone when we call. Both high school and college coaches are just human beings with big professional and personal responsibilities. It is important that we start treating them that way. They very much want you to see them as people who work hard and are trying to make good choices and the best decisions on how to maximize their time and resources…just like you and me.

Still not sure if it's okay to reach out to a college coach? There are nearly eight million student-athletes playing high school sports each year at over 26,000 high schools in 50 states plus the District of Columbia.[7]

---

[7]   NCAA, *"Estimated probability of competing in college athletics,"* https://www.ncaa. org/sports/2015/3/2/estimated-probability-of-competing-in-college-athletics.aspx

The practical question every parent must ask is: *How would a college coach ever find my child when my child is simply another needle in the world's biggest haystack?*

The answer is simple: Invitation.

The best days for a college coach are when a talented student-athlete emails them their on-line profile with their film, grades and contact information and then calls them to express their interest in attending their college and playing for them. Think about what that email and phone call did for that coach. Seventy-five percent of the recruiting process is completed by that email and phone call. The coach doesn't have to find the student-athlete. The coach doesn't have to figure out how to contact them. The coach doesn't have to convince them to look at his or her school. The coach doesn't have to wait weeks or months to receive the information they need to make a proper evaluation of them. The student-athlete did all the heavy lifting for that coach. The only thing that is left to do is figure out if they want to work together and if the school and the coach can provide enough scholarship and/or financial aid to make the school affordable for the family. That will take some time and a lot of effort and patience for both parties, but the student-athlete still went from non-existent to front-and-center recruit in a matter of minutes.

Let's break down the invitation process to its bare-bones parts:

1. Build your on-line profile, which gives you a web address to your very own recruitment website.

2. Find the Head Coach and Assistant Coaches' email addresses and invite them to recruit you. (You will be able to find the email addresses and phone numbers on the

college's website—search for Athletics Directory—or through the recruiting service's website you are using.)

3. Email the full coaching staff a short letter of interest (see template email below) with the link to your on-line profile.

4. Follow up in the next 48 hours with a phone call to the coaching staff, so they can hear your voice and excitement about their school and program (see template voice mail message below).

5. If a week or two go by with no reply, email and call the coaching staff again (see template follow-up email and voice mail below).

If you send two emails with your full profile and leave two voice mails and you still do not get a response, there is a very good chance that they do not have any roster openings for a student-athlete like you or you just are not a good fit for their program. This may hurt a little bit, but you need to see it as a positive. This is one school you can cross off your list, and you can now focus your energy on other schools that may think you are a great fit for them!

INTRODUCTION EMAIL EXAMPLE

To: coachrogers@teachercollege.edu

Cc: asstcoachbob@teachercollege.edu; asstcoachjim@teachercollege.edu

From: jdavis@myhouse.com

Subject: John Davis - 2025 - 6'2" - Point Guard - Small Town, TX - 3.6 GPA/24 ACT

Dear Coach Rogers,

I am writing to let you know that I am very interested in attending Teacher College and playing basketball for you. My dream is to help you win National Championships and graduate with my teaching certificate, so I can teach and coach at the high school level after graduation.

Per my research, my grades and test scores exceed the Admissions standards of your college. I expect both my GPA and ACT scores to improve over the next two years.

I just finished my sophomore year as the starting point guard at Small Town High School in Texas. I average 8 points/game, 4 assists/game and led my team with 80% from the free throw line this season. I helped lead my team to the state playoffs, where we lost by four points to the eventual State Champions. I had 16 points and 5 assists in the final game. I will play for Cowboy Basketball Club this summer. My summer tournament schedule is attached and on my recruiting profile along with my game film and highlight clips and transcripts: Topnotchrecruiting. johndavis.org. It would mean a lot to me if you could make it to one of my games this summer.

I would very much appreciate it if you or one of your assistants would call me back at your convenience. Any feedback on what I can work on to be a better recruit for your program would be greatly appreciated, as well. Please let me know if you are running any summer camps. I would love any opportunity to work with you and your staff to improve my skills going into my junior season.

Thank you for your time and consideration,

John Davis

INTRODUCTION VOICE MAIL EXAMPLE

Hi Coach. My name is John Davis, and I am 6'2" sophomore point guard from Small Town High School in Texas, and I will play for Cowboy Basketball Club this summer. I currently carry a 3.6 GPA and earned a 24 ACT on my first attempt this year. I am calling to express my interest in being recruited to play for your program, and I would appreciate any opportunity to talk to you or your staff on the phone. I emailed you earlier today with my on-line recruiting profile with my film and contact information, but feel free to call me any time at (XXX) XXX-XXXX. If I don't hear back from you, I will try and call again this upcoming Friday after I get home from school around 4 p.m. CST. Have a great day.

FOLLOW-UP EMAIL EXAMPLE

To: coachrogers@teachercollege.edu

Cc: asstcoachbob@teachercollege.edu;   asstcoachjim@teachercollege.edu

From: jdavis@myhouse.com

Subject: 2nd Attempt: John Davis, 2025 PG – Recruit – Small Town, TX

Hi Coach Rogers,

I hope all is well. I am sure you are busy this time of year, but I wanted to follow up from my email and voicemail message I left last Wednesday April 1. I am very excited about the potential of playing for you at Teacher College.

I pride myself on being a leader on and off the court, and I have high expectations that I can lead my team to the State

Championship this year. Here is the link to my on-line recruiting profile if you want to check out my game film and highlights: Topnotchrecruiting.johndavis.org

Thanks again for your time and consideration,

John Davis

FOLLOW-UP VOICE MAIL EXAMPLE

Hi Coach Rogers – this is John Davis again from Small Town High School in Texas. I left you a voice message and sent my profile via email last week, and I was calling to confirm my information was received. I just wanted to let you know how excited I am about the potential of playing for you at Teacher College. If you or your staff have an opportunity to review my information and call me back at your convenience, I would greatly appreciate it. Here is my number again if you need it (XXX) XXX-XXXX. I hope you and your family are doing well. Have a great day.

The keys to a great invitation through email or call are:

1. Give the college coaches the facts about you; keep it brief and to the point

2. Be positive and demonstrate enthusiasm

3. Always ask for a response or a reply

4. Make sure it is clear that you will follow up

The worst thing that can happen by reaching out to a college coach and expressing your interest in being recruited is that they tell you they are not interested or no longer recruiting your class. What's the worst thing that can happen if you don't reach out to a college coach? They recruit someone else instead of you because you didn't take five minutes to introduce yourself. Let that sink in!

A College Coach's Perspective

Email is definitely the best way to initially reach out to a college coach. Be sure to include: graduation year, name, height, position, highlight film, academic interests, and phone number.

An ideal time to make initial contact is your freshmen or sophomore year. At that time, NCAA D3, NAIA, and NCAA D2 institutions are typically working on the class a year or two older than you, so don't be surprised if you don't hear back from those coaches immediately. However, some non-NCAA D1 coaches do start their recruiting classes early (we do), and some run camps in the spring/summer and would add you to their invitation list. Camps are a great way to get on a college's radar early!

For most coaches, the recruiting process is about being as efficient as possible. College coaches don't want to waste your time, and they don't want you wasting their time. Do your research on schools before reaching out to the coach. Don't send blanket emails to every school you can think of without knowing if they even offer your major.

You wouldn't want a school to lead you on with no intention of offering you a spot on their team, and college coaches don't want to think that you are a recruitable athlete if their school doesn't even check half of your priority boxes.

Oliver Wiseman

Head Women's Basketball Coach, Benedictine University

- 3 NCAA National Tournament Appearances
- 8 Years as a NCAA D3 and D2 Assistant Coach

Chapter 7: Action Steps

- Choose at least four to five schools from your Attack List each month.

- Email your interest and on-line profile to the Head Coach AND their assistants.

- Follow up with another email and phone call within 2 weeks if they do not respond.

Chapter 8:
Increase Your Value through Competition

I have been up against tough competition all my life;
I wouldn't know how to get along without it.

- Walt Disney

As we begin Chapter 8, you should feel over-the-moon good. Look at all the things you probably didn't have when you first cracked open this playbook.

You now have an on-line profile to make you immensely more visible to college coaches. You have an individualized Attack List of schools that fit your needs and ability. You know how to invite college coaches to you, the right way, by making the coach's job easier to recruit you. You are no longer setting lofty goals without a plan to accomplish those goals. You know the importance of asking the right questions to make sure you are pinpointing the right colleges and universities, and you are not wasting your time or the time of coaches at schools that simply don't fit your needs and priorities.

If you have followed the first seven chapters of this playbook, you now have the tools and knowledge to communicate with coaches TODAY! Remember, the earlier you begin, the earlier coaches are looking at you instead of the thousands of other recruits very similar to you.

You have come a long way! You've earned the right to be extremely proud of yourself. Most student-athletes who have the ability to play in college never get to this stage because they didn't have the information you now have to do it and do it right!

Now that you're ready to reach out to college coaches and invite them to evaluate you, it is essential that you understand what those coaches want to see.

College coaches want to see recruits in their element being the best version of themselves, and they want to see you compete against high level competition as much as possible. In this Chapter, I will give you a general idea of what to prepare for when building competition film/video, but also what those coaches want to see when they watch you compete live.

For multi-sport athletes, I will dive into the challenges you will face with your visibility strategies but also the many positives that you should embrace.

Let's start with film/video because I've talked too vaguely about film for too many chapters, and besides your grades, it is the most important element coaches will ask about. You need to understand it and be very competent in how you demonstrate your abilities on film.

In general, whether coaches are watching your film or they're at your event watching you compete live, they are looking for very specific attributes, no matter your sport:

- Respect: Do you respect the game, your teammates and coaches, officials and opponents?

- Energy: Does your energy go up and down or does it stay consistent throughout the contest? Can you find that "extra" speed or focus when your team needs a little bit more from you?

- Teamwork: Do you work well with others and contribute to the team concept? Do you support your teammates no matter if you are winning or losing?

- IQ: Do you understand the game and demonstrate the instincts to read, react and adapt?

What type of film does a coach want to see from Basketball, Football, Field Hockey, Ice Hockey, Lacrosse, Soccer, Volleyball, Wrestling and Water Polo recruits?

- Game/competition film against strong competition

- Speed

- Size

- Agility

- Exceptional skill

- Special/difference-making qualities

What type of film does a coach want to see from Baseball, Golf, Softball and Tennis recruits?

- Skill footage. Practice instead of competition footage.

- A disciplined repetition of skills. What does your swing, pitch or defense look like 20 to 30 times in a row?

What type of film does a coach want to see from Cross-country, Rowing, Swimming and Diving, and Track and Field?

- Stats, stats, stats (times and distances mean everything)

- These are the only sports where a coach will get excited about your potential without seeing you compete live or on film. For example, if you can run a 10 second 100-meter dash, you are worth a phone call.

- Coaches still want to see your film. Both skill/practice footage and competition footage are equally good for these sports. Rowers should show three to five minutes on an ERG or 10 minutes in the boat. Cross-country runners should show the first 100 to 200 meters and the last 100 to 200 meters of a race or two.

If you are a team sport recruit, I recommend posting at least one full game for coaches to see. College coaches understand that highlight films can be manipulated to make you look like you never make a mistake. Coaches know that is not the case. They want to see how you react when things are not going well. Keep your highlight films to a maximum of three to five minutes, but I would also include at least one full game for them to evaluate your character, ability and energy throughout a game. Don't worry if the film shows you are not a starter. There have been many professional draft picks who never started a game in college. Coaches are looking for talent and fit. They understand that your high school coach may have to use you differently than they plan on using you. If you have talent that makes the coach excited about you, then it doesn't matter if you start or come off the bench.

How important is playing for a club or travel team in the off-season?

It really depends on which college coach you ask. Most college coaches will tell you that they are not big fans of travel/club teams, but they see it as a necessary part of the recruiting process.

Let's say you are a high school softball player. You play about 15 to 20 high school games per year between March and May. Let's say I am a college softball coach. My team plays 50 games from February to June. My team practices and plays on the same days and times that your team plays. When do I come watch you play?

If you play on a travel/club team from May to July, my season is typically over by early June, so I have time to travel to tournaments anywhere in the country during the summer. As a college softball coach, I will use June and July to watch 90% of my recruits live, and that may be the only time I will get to do so.

For this reason, travel/club competition can be a necessity for many families and many coaches. Often, the high school team is in such a small community with very little competition that travel/club opportunities are the only times a recruit can compete against high level talent and perhaps for the first time get high level collegiate-type coaching and instruction.

My daughter is a multi-sport athlete who plays volleyball in the fall, basketball in the winter and softball in the spring. She doesn't have the time to do club or travel ball. Is that a bad thing?

Absolutely not! It is a great thing. A gentleman by the name of Mark Rerick wrote a great piece a few years back called "The Importance of Multi-sport Participation" that sums up the debate as well as any I have read on the topic.[8] The essay basically says that being a multi-sport athlete has numerous short and long-term benefits including but not limited to:

1. Multi-sport athletes are healthier and happier throughout their adult lives

2. Multi-sport athletes are less injury prone

3. Multi-sport athletes are better teammates and more adaptable to coaching

4. Multi-sport athletes don't quit. They continue to play their sports through high school and college more often, and much more often into their adult lives

I know many parents have had to face difficult decisions because their child loves playing more than one sport. **Don't ever let anyone convince you that is a bad thing.** College coaches love multi-sport athletes for all the reasons above. When travel/club competition is not possible, the first seven chapters of this playbook become even more essential, including a strong online presence and a consistent updating of film.

I highly recommend that families who do not have the ability to put their child on travel/club teams use the summers to get ultra-focused on one to two college camps at colleges and universities their child has on their Attack List. College coaches who like what they see in your child's film would love the op-

---

8   Rerick, Mark, "The Importance of Multi-sport Participation," *NFHS.org*, *https://www.nfhs.org/articles/the-importance-of-multi-sport-participation/* (published June 1, 2016)

portunity to work with your child on their campus for a few days. Often, that time to coach a recruit is much more valuable than watching them play live coached by someone else.

Think about this from a financial perspective. Most clubs will cost anywhere from $2,000 to $5,000 per year and that is before the parents pay for travel, food and housing to attend all the tournaments. A family dropping $10,000 per year for their child to play travel/club sports has unfortunately become the norm, and unless the club has scholarships or sponsors, it is almost impossible for low-income families to pay for a travel/club team.

There are a lot of college/university camps where you may pay $200 to $600 for a week of instruction with college coaches. Two to three of those camps every summer is a lot cheaper than playing for a travel/club team.

The key is still the invitation. Let college coaches know that you are a multi-sport athlete, so playing for a club is not possible. Ask them to evaluate your film and ask them if they see enough potential that a week of camp with them on their campus would be as valuable as or more valuable than spending a lot of money to see you play at a summer tournament.

In the end, it all goes back to a strong on-line resume, good film and the invitation. Those three actions open the doors to having personal and productive conversations with coaches. It is amazing what will happen when a college coach likes you. **Many obstacles can be overcome just by saying "Hi, I'm interested in you. I'd like to know if you'd be interested in me."**

Carpe diem. Seize the day! Whether coaches see you on film or live really doesn't matter. The key is finding a way for them to see your ability. Sometimes we must get creative, but hopefully this chapter has opened your eyes to your reality and how to make the most of it.

A College Coach's Perspective

For me, seeing a recruit play is the most important aspect of the recruiting process. I prefer to watch recruits play live because I then get a better understanding of how they interact with their coaches, teammates, opposing players and officials. I have passed on many players in my career because of bad body language and negative interactions on the court.

However, we tend to be more successful in getting out-of-area players, so I rely heavily on video as well. I prefer highlight videos, but I also like to watch game film, preferably a good half. I rarely watch an entire game unless I am in attendance live. (Note: If you send a coach game film, send a game where you do some good things early. Don't send a game where you play poorly for a first half because the college coach might not watch the good second half.)

As far as the high school vs. AAU argument is concerned, I am fine with either, although I would slightly lean towards high school games. However, I realize that it is often easier for me to see an AAU game. One thing I look for is the talent level of the team they're playing against. I want to see a recruit play against good opposition that forces them to play at a high level.

Chris Bunch

Head Men's Basketball Coach, Webster University

- Winningest Men's Basketball Coach in Webster University history
- 8 Conference Titles
- 3 Conference Tournament Titles
- 3 NCAA Tournament appearances (2011, 2014 and 2020)

Chapter 8: Action Steps

- Compete as much as possible against the best competition possible
- Film your practices, games and events
- Update film of you playing on your on-line profile every month

Chapter 9:
Utilize the Good of Social Media and Marketing

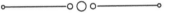

Social media is not media. It's a conversation.

- David Alston

John was one of the best kids I ever assessed and mentored. In Chapter 3, I told Thomas's story and how he was doing almost everything wrong in his process. John was the exact opposite. John was doing everything right.

John's family was not wealthy by any means. Neither parent had a four-year college degree, but both had worked blue-collar jobs in a small town, raising their kids with a value system focused on respect, hard work, and education. John's parents wanted their kids to have the type of education their parents were unable to provide for them.

John was a three-sport star. Earning First Team accolades in any sport is a great accomplishment. John was First Team All-Conference in all three sports. He was Senior Class President, a National Honor Society member, a 3.8 student with a 27 ACT, a great big brother to his three younger siblings, and his parents made sure he went to church every Sunday. When I got on the phone with him and his parents for the first time, he immediately made me smile:

"Hi Coach Rogers. Thank you for taking the time to talk with me and my parents. My dream is to play college basketball, and we really do not know what we are doing. We need all the help you are willing to give us."

Wow! All I had said before this came out of his mouth was, "Hello John and parents."

In 10 seconds of talking to this kid, I was immediately ready to climb the highest mountain and swim the longest sea to help him. He was passionate, humble, articulate, generous, and kind. It was obvious why he was named Team Captain by his teammates and coaches on all three of his teams.

At the end of our conversation that night I remember giving him the best compliment I can give a young man.

"John, I have a young son. If he grows up to have half of the conviction and character that you have, I will be one very proud dad."

I meant every word, and I mean it to this day. He was the perfect recruit. A person who had never coached or recruited in their life could have gotten this young man recruited. That's why the next part of his story is hard for me to tell, but it's the story every student-athlete needs to hear.

As you can imagine, John did everything my team and I laid out for him. He followed every direction and completed every task in a timely manner. He was not a good enough athlete to play at the Division I level, but that was never his goal. He just wanted a great education and a place where he could continue to play a significant role on a team for four years while earning his degree. His parents wanted him to attend a school with a Christian foundation.

John had no problem with his recruitment. He ended up having over 400 college coaches look at his on-line profile, and he ended up committing early in his senior year to a great NAIA program with a Christian focus. John's grades and test scores were good enough that after he received an academic scholarship and an institutional grant, his parents only had about $8,000 to pay out of pocket. The Head Coach at this school took care of that with an $8,000 annual basketball scholarship. John had built himself the ideal 3-Legged Stool, and in return, his entire education was now paid for.

John went on to have his best season as a senior. He led the conference in scoring and helped his team advance deep into the State Tournament. He took nothing for granted. He continued to get straight A's in both his final semesters, and he even re-took the ACT to jump his score up to a 29. When I asked him why he re-took the test when he already had his full ride in his pocket, he said, "I just knew I could do better, Coach, and I had to prove it to myself."

I wish I was making this kid up. He would make a great fictional character, but this young man was the real deal.

John never drank a drop of alcohol in his young life and no drug had ever entered his body outside of a few Advil to get through football season. His parents thought social media was a terrible waste of time and energy, but they let him create a Twitter account his senior year because some college coaches had told him that they were on Twitter, and it was a good way for them to follow him and communicate with him through the recruiting process. I don't think John ever posted anything on Twitter outside of a few pictures of himself and his teammates and family.

As John prepared for his high school graduation in late May, there was a huge weight beginning to lift off his shoulders. He had sacrificed a lot to get where he was. He had completely focused his 18 years of life on four things: faith, family, academics, and the sports that he loved. He had never really compromised that focus or those values. Even the girlfriend he had throughout high school understood that she was fifth on that list, and I think that made her like John even more. She was an equally great kid and student.

John also knew that he took a huge weight off his parents' shoulders. As the oldest child in the family, he knew what that full ride meant to the family budget. Although he was a great role model for his siblings, he knew the odds of his siblings getting the opportunity to go to college for free would be nearly impossible, so the money he was saving his parents was going to go a long way toward his parents being able to send all four kids to a good college. Of all his accomplishments, I think he was most proud of that.

As his high school graduation neared, his best friends started to nag him about being so tight-vested, and now that he had his future locked up, they encouraged him to loosen up and come to the pre-graduation party one of their friends was throwing out in the country at an old farmhouse. John agreed that he had earned the right to have a little fun like the rest of his classmates, and he asked his parents if it would be okay, just this once, if he went out to the party that upcoming Friday night. He assured them that he had no interest in abandoning his conviction and beliefs about alcohol and drugs, and he would be home by 11pm. After some very lengthy conversations, his parents relented and agreed to let him go.

John was thrilled. He felt like he could finally let his hair down a bit and be a kid. He wanted to get a glimpse of how the other side of the fence looked and felt.

John got to the party around 7pm, and the whole house erupted when John walked through the door. No one could believe that John had actually come to a party. There weren't many people in his small town that didn't love him. They had all cheered for him. He was the reason that their boys' sports teams were so successful, and the kids at the party were excited that they finally got to celebrate their life-long journey and his personal successes together. John was immediately happy with his decision to go to the party. He felt vindicated for talking his parents into it.

Although he was having fun, he was still ultra-focused on what was happening around him. There was alcohol being consumed throughout the house and outside. He didn't know what exactly he was smelling, but he knew there were people smoking somewhere. Although many classmates tried to convince him to drink a beer with them, John didn't budge and kept a red Solo cup full of lemonade in his hand all night. He knew there was no alcohol in his cup, but he was okay if no one else knew that. He just wanted to fit in for one night without being called a *prude* or *lame*. He'd heard that enough over the past four years. Tonight, he was going to have fun, but he was going to do it his way.

Around 10:30pm, John quietly said goodbye to a few close friends and snuck out of the house and drove his dad's truck back home. As he walked in the door to his family home a few minutes before 11pm, his parents breathed a quiet sigh of relief. They, too, now felt vindicated for trusting in their son. He told them a little about the party, and he thanked his parents for letting him go. He had a lot of fun, and he did it the right way. They all slept well that night, and John fell asleep with a big smile on his face.

About two weeks after the party, I received a phone call from John. I could immediately tell he was upset. His voice was shaky, and it sounded like he had been crying. I had never heard this version of John. Every hair on my body stood up. The only thing I could think of was that one his parents or siblings had died. I was immediately prepared for the worst.

I calmly said, "John, what's wrong. Are you and your family okay?"

It took him a few seconds, but he found his composure and said, "I lost my scholarship. Can you help me?"

He went on to tell me that he had received a call from the Head Coach at the university that had loved him, recruited him and signed him. The coach told him that his staff monitors all their present players and their recruits' social media accounts, and he was very disappointed when his staff had brought it to his attention that there were pictures of John on-line at a party where alcohol was everywhere including in what looked like in John's hand.

It seems one of John's classmates had taken a picture of John with his three best friends at the party. None of them had any alcohol in their hands, but all had red Solo cups in their hands, and in the background on the kitchen table there were clear signs of beer cans and bottles of alcohol. The classmate who had taken the picture had posted it on her social media account and tagged John and his friends. He remembered the picture, but he did not give anyone the okay to post his picture on-line.

John told the coach that he had not been drinking that night or any night. He was enjoying being with his best friends (who were also not drinking) at a pre-graduation party to celebrate their last year together.

The coach went on to tell John how strict his university's alcohol and drug policy was at his school. John had remembered the coach explaining the zero-tolerance policy this Christian school had in their campus student policy and procedure hand-book, and he had no problems with it. He didn't think much about it because he thought he would never have any interest in challenging those rules in any way.

John was devastated. He had done nothing wrong. In fact, he had gone out of his way in an environment full of tempta-tion, to be the best version of himself.

By the time John had called me, it was the first week of June. Ninety-nine percent of the four-year programs had filled their rosters and offered all their scholarships, and the 1% who may have taken John at that point would have cost John's family much too much out-of-pocket for them to even consider it.

We were able to get John to a local junior college where the family only had to pay about $1000 per semester for him to attend. He was able to play for two years, and he then transferred to a D3 to finish up his degree. If you just focus on his four years of college, John had a great college career. He still played ball for four years. He walked away with an outstanding degree. He left college the same young man he entered college—as the type of person we all hope our children will grow up being. John's story is not a sad one when you look at it from that perspective.

However, what you need to understand from John's situation is that his parents ended up having to pay about $15,000 out of pocket to get him through college, and John had to take an extra $20,000 in student loans to offset the family expense. That $35,000 in cost was supposed to be $0. John also had to attend schools that were not the best fit for him compared to what his work throughout high school should have earned him. That one night and that one picture and that one innocent tag on social media by a friend with nothing but good intentions in her heart had cost John and his family the future they had imagined and worked so hard for.

After reading this, you might think that I am the biggest anti-social media person you have ever met. Fifteen years ago, you would have been correct. Instead of me giving you my opinions on social media, I think it is more important that you have a firm understanding of the do's and don'ts of social media, and then make the best decisions for you and your family.

THE DO's

- Utilize Facebook, Twitter, Instagram, Tik Tok, etc., to allow coaches to get to know you.

- Post positive things about yourself and your team.

- Re-post quotes, articles, statements that demonstrate your values and core beliefs.

- Post pictures of yourself with family and friends in positive situations that demonstrate your depth as a person.

- Post the link to your on-line recruiting profile.

- Post video clips of you training or short snippets of great plays in your games or events.

- Respond in a timely manner when a college coach contacts you. [If a coach sends you a message, and you do not respond for three to four weeks, you are basically telling them that you are not interested, and they should move on to other recruits.]

THE DON'Ts

- Do not post inappropriate pictures or use inappropriate language in tweets or posts — including retweets.

- Do not speak poorly about your teammates, other schools, or the students at other schools.

- Do not speak ill of anyone.

- Do not insert yourself in controversial conversations or engage in arguments.

- Stay away from politics and religion.

- Immediately delete/block those who post things on your account who do not represent you in a positive nature.

- Make sure your friends are not "tagging" you in pictures or situations that could bring your character into question.

- Do not post while emotions are running high.

- Do not post anything that you would not want mom, dad, grandma or grandpa to see or read.

If you feel like you can stay true to these principles, I encourage you to use and enjoy the good of social media. Always keep John's story tucked away in the back of your brain, though. Social media can be like a long, beautiful walk along a mountain trail. It may be a fun, healthy experience, but you must be ever cognizant of the wild animals that are out there with you who do not have your best interests at heart.

MARKETING

At this point in the Marketing and Social Media chapter, you may be saying to yourself, *Is that all there is to marketing—social media? Coach Rogers hasn't used the word marketing once in this chapter.* You would be right, I have not discussed the word marketing once this chapter, but if you think back, I have been touching on marketing in each and every chapter. It seems that whenever I speak at a school or host a webinar, social media seems to take over the marketing discussion, and I can go down that rabbit hole with my audience. Social media is such a small part of recruitment marketing, but it is far and away the most controversial.

Let's refresh your memory on how much we have already discussed marketing:

- All of you should have an on-line recruiting profile on a site with lots of college coach traffic and visibility (see Chapter 5)

- All prospective recruits should be emailing their letter of interest and the link to their on-line profile to at least four new college coaches each month (Chapter 7)

- Recruits need to keep their high school, club game, tournament, summer camp, and showcase schedule updated on their respective on-line profiles, so coaches can see, at their convenience, when and where they can go watch you play and compete (Chapter 5)

- List your social media sites on your on-line profile and copy and paste your on-line profile link to the bio section of your social media profiles and channels (Chapters 5 and 9).

If you are going to have a social media presence, I encourage you to follow and direct message coaches at the schools on your Attack List through those social media sites. Add that to your monthly to-do list. When you email and call a coach to invite them to recruit you, simply hop on your social media and follow and message the coaches you happened to email and call that day.

The only big marketing piece that we haven't discussed is your club and high school coaches. Although I shifted the recruitment responsibility away from your coaches in Chapter 7, your coaches can still play a significant role in your recruitment if (1) they want to help you, and (2) you want them to help you. I know relationships with coaches can sometimes be tricky, so use your coaches to your advantage as much as you feel comfortable doing so. For example, ask your coach if they would be willing to call four college coaches for you per month. Ask your coach to call the same ones you are going to email and call. Sometimes a college coach appreciates having a conversation with a recruit's high school or club coach, so they can ask about character and work ethic, and hear if the recruit's present coach is excited about coaching you.

At the end of the day, this entire playbook is a marketing education book. If I was a Marketing Executive, it would be important that I know the value of the product I am marketing before I think about how I want to market it. You are the CEO or Marketing Executive of your own company now. How you are perceived is the foundation of a good marketing strategy. You should now have a very firm grasp of what coaches are looking for and how to present yourself to coaches in the most respectful and flattering ways.

One last thing on marketing and film: I have had literally thousands of kids who have sent me their highlight videos with music overtop of the video that the recruit thought was motivating and would help the college coach watching the film get even more excited about watching them play.

I always ask these recruits:

"What if the coach you are sending this to does not like the rap or rock or country music that you love? What if your music choice negatively affects their first impression of you?"

"Well, I didn't think about that. I just figured they would like some music instead of just watching my boring game film."

What kids and a lot of parents don't understand is that coaches are typically only going to watch three to five minutes of film before deciding if you go in the "keep" or "discard" pile. They want to be focused on your ability and not your choice of music or the slow motion effects you added. Give them the plain Jane film. You can talk musical tastes and your film editing skills once you are on the team!

In the end, marketing begins with the invitation and progresses with you consistently, month-to-month, keeping your profile updated and continuing to grow your leverage. Don't be afraid to get creative, but I would always go back to the "do's and don'ts" listed above in the social media section. The answers to those questions will always guide you to make good decisions.

A College Coach's Perspective

Social media plays an interesting role in the recruitment process. It helps coaches and future teammates get a glimpse into who the prospective student athlete is, who they want to become, what they value, and how they like to tell their story. What I've also learned is that this glimpse into a student-athlete's life is only a small portion of what makes that individual unique, and our coaching staff approaches social media with a healthy amount of investigation. With multiple touch points throughout the recruitment process, the social media profile curated by a student-athlete plays a similar role to a book cover, enticing the reader to pick it up and learn more about what the chapters have to offer.

If social media is a tool recruits would like to use, my best advice is the same advice I give to our current players about operating their personal accounts:

1. **Be Authentic** – Have a healthy relationship with social media. Be proud of who you are and your book cover. I don't ever want my players to try and be someone they are not. We all know how social media has played a role in mental health and how mental health can play a big role in success on the court. Learning to be authentic helps with the latter.

2. **Be Appropriate** – Don't turn away viewers! Most high schoolers think of their audience as their friends. They post to engage that age bracket. Once you have stepped into the recruiting world, your audience changes, and so you must change how you portray your story. This is also what leads me to my third point because there are many different perceptions of how to define the word appropriate.

3. **Find a Proofreader** – For our team the proofreader is our captains because they have had years of evidence to show they understand how to create a proper social media platform. For a recruit it can be a club coach, parent, recruiting service, etc. Essentially someone who is older and already in the professional world. If they see something posted that seems questionable, give them space to give you feedback. The way a picture or post is perceived may be different than what you intended. A proofreader helps your impact meet your intention.

4. **Control Your Story** because it is only for you to tell. Keep up with privacy settings and set controls, so no one can tag you without your permission.

The truth is, I've read plenty of great books with bad covers and plenty of terrible books with great covers. My hope is by reading this book and finding a great team, you can figure out how to write a best-selling story that's accompanied by a great book cover.

Samantha Birkicht

Head Women's Volleyball Coach, University of Wisconsin-Platteville

- 7 Seasons as a Head College Coach
- 5 Seasons as an Assistant College Coach
- 2 Seasons as a Head High School Coach
- 6 Seasons as a Volleyball Club Director

Chapter 9: Action Steps

- If you are going to have a social media account, focus all entries on your recruitment and demonstrating your character and strong academics.

- Marketing is about routine and consistency. Focus on reaching out to four new college coaches per month and follow up with each by the end of that month.

- Be responsive when college coaches reach out to you.

Chapter 10:
Stay on Top of Your Game

Many of life's failures are people who did not know
how close they were when they gave up.

- Thomas Edison

Sophomore twins Derek and Mark were my only returning starters from our State Championship team. We had just graduated six seniors, two of which were First Team All-State and the third was Honorable Mention All-State and First Team All-Conference. We were graduating about 60 points per game and a ton of athleticism, leadership and confidence. Most people I talked to after the season simply assumed that we were going to greatly struggle the next season. We were losing too much fire power in the graduating senior class. I usually nodded and agreed that we were graduating a lot of talent, but I kept the two aces I had up my sleeve to myself.

The twins were blue-collar gym rats. They LOVED playing basketball. I couldn't get them out of the gym. At 6-4 and 6-5 respectively (they would eventually grow to 6-7 and 6-8), they were skinny as rails and growing like weeds, but they both had a tremendous hunger to get better and a great desire to be great. They were the types of kids you dreamed about coaching.

The problem was that as our championship season progressed the previous season, the opposition coaches were starting to see that both boys were very one-dimensional. Derek, the lefty, always went left and Mark, the righty, always went right. You could force either one to their opposite hand, and there was a good chance that something bad would happen.

If I expected these two young bucks to take over the scoring and leadership load of our program and lead us back to another State Championship, I needed to break them of some very bad habits and help them turn their glaring weaknesses into exceptional strengths. For Derek and Mark, that meant I had to teach them both how to be equally competent with both their natural strong hand and their evidently weak off hand.

We weren't going to accomplish this type of growth only working one to two times per week. For most kids, that was a two- to three-year journey. Derek and Mark were not *most* kids. They met me at the gym every single morning that summer. I know we usually took a weekend day off, but there were very few days where the three of us were not training and improving.

I remember we were finishing up our first individual workout with the two of them that off-season when I asked them how committed they were to learning how to be great players and leading us to a second championship. They both made it very clear to me that they had no other intention. Not only did they want to win more championships, but they also had very real aspirations of being D1 recruits and playing college ball.

I told them that the key to accomplishing all their goals didn't start in the gym. It started as soon as they walked out the gym doors. They were confused and clearly skeptical.

I said, "Derek, your number one goal this summer is to become right-handed, and Mark, your number one goal is to become left-handed." They both gave me a funny look, and Derek said, "Haven't we been doing that already, Coach? You've been having us do every drill with both our right and left hands."

I said, "Yes, you are not wrong. What we do in the gym, and how we do it is still very important, but when you walk out of here today, I want you to do everything with your weak hands. Derek, I want you opening every door with your right hand. I want you to eat cereal and brush your teeth and scratch the back of your head when you have an itch with your right hand. Anything you normally do with your strong hand, I now want you to use only your weak hand. Mark, I want you to do the same, but always with your left hand."

I could see their brains working a thousand miles an hour, and finally I got a smile out of them. "Will that really work?" Mark asked.

I said, "Not only is it going to work, but it is going to make you the best basketball players in the State, and it is going to be the reason you both will go to college for free."

What both boys didn't understand is how naturally un-balanced the typical human being is. Someone who is truly ambidextrous is considered an anomaly in our world. It is true that a small number of our population are born with a natural inclination to use both hands and both feet equally, but that natural ability is very rare. For those of us *not* born with the ability, it can be taught, and it can be an enormous advantage for those who take learning of that skill seriously.

Derek and Mark didn't just take my challenge seriously. They embraced it like it was the oxygen they needed to breathe. Within three weeks, they were doing every drill I gave them with the same dexterity in both hands. I was also able to teach them and train them to shoot free throws and jump shots with their "weak" hands. They were quickly becoming players with no weaknesses that an opposing coach could pinpoint and attack.

Not only did their work open their brains to another level of capability, but it had also opened an entire side of the basketball court that they were now learning to dominate and own. They were learning how to be progressively great, and more days than not, when they walked out of the gym each day, they were exceptionally better than the day before.

By that winter, we were back to being ranked near the top of the State. We had D1 coaches come to watch the twins practice as often as they could get to us. We ended up losing by three points in the Regional Championship Game to the team that would end up winning the State Championship. We finished the season 21-7. It was all because Derek and Mark had committed to working to become the very best versions of themselves and being honest about their weaknesses. Significance!

Both young men went on to punch their D1 ticket and go to college under full scholarship. Both Derek and Mark would go overseas and make a great living as professional basketball players. They made their dreams come true because they never stopped learning and developing their physical and emotional capabilities.

Progressive Development

Merriam-Webster defines *progressive* as "making use of or interested in new ideas, findings, or opportunities; moving forward or onward; *advancing.*"

Parents, I encourage you to challenge your child to be progressive in their development.

The first time a college coach calls your child, it won't be to make them an offer. As we have learned in previous chapters, it will be to start building a relationship with your child, and to find out if they have the ability and desire to grow and get better. Why would any coach recruit a player who had already reached their peak as an athlete or recruit someone who had become content with their ability?

As a parent, the worst thing we can do is force our kids to learn or work hard at something. We must think like the character Elliot in my favorite scene from the movie *E.T. The Extra-Terrestrial.* We must leave our kids a trail of metaphorical Reece's Pieces, so they have daily motivation to find that learning and work ethic on their own.

That's great, Coach Rogers. Easier said than done. I can barely get my kid out of bed in the morning to get to school on time. How do we accomplish this trail of motivation?

As you already know, I am sure, the right trail of motivation is different for every student-athlete. As parents and coaches, we must be as progressive and creative with our parenting and coaching as we hope our kids will be with their learning and development. Below is a list of ways to get them inspired. I am confident that you are already doing some of these things. Whether you are utilizing these tools and methods or not, the important thing is to keep trying. Kids find their motivation at different times and in different ways. At one point, they will sink their hooks into something and make it their own.

Here are some ways you can encourage and motivate your child toward progressive learning and development:

- *Play with your child.* You don't have to be good enough to train them or coach them, but can you play catch after dinner a few nights per week? Can you rebound when they shoot baskets? Can you take them to a batting cage or mini-golf park and just have fun competing as a family?

- *Take them to high level contests.* Get tickets to go watch the local college or pro team play. Call local college coaches to see if they would be open to you and your child coming to campus to watch a practice. I would never say "no" to a parent who wanted to bring their child to my practice.

- *Send YouTube and Instagram videos* to your kids of inspirational quotes, speeches, trainings or game/event clips that caught your attention. Your kids might not think everything you send them is as special as you do, but it only takes one to get them to want more or to want to talk about what you just sent.

- *Create a monthly practice/training calendar togethe*r. It is amazing how much weight I lost when I started weighing myself each day and tracking my weight, so I could witness my progress. It is amazing what happens if there is a calendar in the house that clearly states when your child has committed to training and then checking off the box each day when the training is completed.

- *Encourage your kids to find older, better athletes to work out with and train.*

- *Work out with your child.* Can you commit to doing three sets of 10 push-ups and three sets of 20 crunches together each night before you go to bed?

- *Sign up for the local 5k races.* You don't even have to run them, but what happens if you walk the 5k together and finish it together?

- *Watch professional athlete and coach interviews together.* Listen to their words. Their struggles. Their motivations. Their fears. Show your child that even the best athletes are not perfect, but they have a desire to put the effort in to be the best versions of themselves.

- *Set weekly and monthly goals together.* We are going to run five miles per week or walk 20 miles per month together.

- *Make sure they are setting athletic baselines* for their sport and athleticism and working to beat their personal bests. "In May, I maxed out my bench press at 160 lbs. I am going to focus on maxing out at 170 pounds by the end of June." "Last week during training, I was able to field 20 ground balls cleanly before mis-fielding a ground ball. This week, I am going to shoot for cleanly fielding 25 ground balls in a row each afternoon before I leave the field."

- ***Inspire a progressive attitude about academics***: "Last semester I got four A's, one B+ and one B. My goal this semester is to have at least five A's and nothing lower than a B+."

- ***Encourage your kids to squeeze a tennis ball in each hand*** while you are watching TV after dinner or do 10 finger-tip push-ups during commercials. Squeezing tennis balls for four to five minutes each day and doing finger-tip push-ups three to four times per week can do amazing things for their hand strength.

- ***Challenge your kids to hold a plank*** during commercial breaks while watching TV. Planks are one of the best things kids can do to increase their core strength. Not only will it improve their athleticism, but it can greatly decrease back, leg and core injuries.

- ***Let them know how they can improve their weaknesses***: "I'm going to brush my teeth with my weak hand for two weeks straight to improve my weaknesses and overall muscle memory and coordination."

As a college coach, I loved it when I called a recruit and that recruit could list off their training schedule and regimen. It told me so much about them when they were excited to tell me about what they'd been doing, watching and learning…especially if they had an excitement in their voice about goals they had set and met or exceeded.

It tells me everything about a player if they are excited about growth and development. I can always tell if a kid is trying to convince me of something or if they are just extraordinarily proud of what they are doing. I can never have enough of kids who are simply excited about getting better.

Persistence

So many families I talk to have a great fear of rubbing a coach the wrong way by being overbearing. I very much respect the empathy families have for college coaches; however, it can sometimes be that family's downfall. Never be afraid to email a coach five to six months after emailing and calling for the first time. Rosters change every day. You never know when a college coach is going to lose a player to injury or transfer or a family issue or financial situation.

As you recall from Chapter 4, I gave you the four actions steps that your child needs to consistently accomplish each month. Here's a recap:

Monthly Action Goals

1. Keep making your grades and test scores your priority to improve each semester

2. Build an on-line recruitment profile and update that profile at least once a month

3. Choose at least 50 to 100 colleges (five to 10 per month) you want to invite to recruit you

4. Email your on-line profile and interest to at least four to five new college coaches per month

Persistence is the key to your success moving forward. Let's say it is January 1 and your son/daughter is a high school freshman, and they have expressed their commitment to playing college tennis. They have good grades and are working every semester to maintain and improve those grades. You have also scheduled them to take their first SAT during the summer between their freshman and sophomore years. Their profile is 80% complete, and they have favorited 60 schools on their recruiting site that they want to reach out to. Make sure they are updating their profile with new film, report cards, game schedules, etc., so any time a coach wants to check in on them, they have new ways of evaluating your child and watching them improve.

Your son/daughter is going to use the template I gave them in Chapter 7 to email five coaches a month from their favorites (Attack List). That means by the following January, they will have emailed 60 college coaches (five emails x 12 months = 60 invites). Your child is determined to play at the D1 level, so among the 60 invites, 30 have been to D1 coaches, 10 have been to D2 coaches, 10 have been to NAIA coaches, and 10 have been to D3 coaches. He or she is focused on their dream schools, but they are putting their eggs in multiple baskets so they have multiple backup plans.

Per NCAA rules, the D1 and the D2 coaches cannot respond to your son/daughter's emails until after their sophomore year is completed, but many of the coaches will send generic camp invites or questionnaires to fill out to let them know that they are getting their information.

D3 and NAIA coaches will respond to their emails (D3 and NAIA coaches can have full contact with recruits at the start of their freshmen year of high school). They will thank your son/daughter for their interest in their program, they will tell your son/daughter that they have their information in their database, and they will encourage them to keep in touch with their progress.

This is where you do not want to get complacent. If you are on a recruiting site, your son/daughter is also starting to get looks and communication from coaches not on their Attack List. Your child needs to be researching these schools and always responding to those coaches. Don't forget what you have learned. You never know when one of your top options is going to drop out of contention. You must remember to continually be thinking about your leverage, so you can be in control of your situation. Additionally, you never want to burn a bridge with a coach who is interested in you just because they are at a school you aren't interested in.

The Persistent Recruit

I recruited Brad as hard as I've ever recruited any student-athlete. I got to watch him play at a camp I was coaching at during the summer before his junior year, and I fell in love with his ability and character almost immediately. I sent him personal letters and drove up to Wisconsin multiple times to do home visits. We built a great relationship, but he ended up choosing a school that was able to give him a bigger financial aid and scholarship package than my school was able to give. Although I was disappointed to not be able to coach Brad, I was confident that he was making the best decision for himself and his family. Over the years, Brad would call me periodically and ask about me, my family and my team. It was always great to hear from him, and he always expressed regret that he chose the scholarship over playing for me. I had mixed emotions to hear those things because I want every kid to have a great college experience, and I assured him that his choices were made for the right reasons. I respected him immensely, and I was very happy that he was still in my life.

After graduating from college, Brad built a relationship with a very famous professional athlete, and he eventually went to work for this pro athlete running his charity foundation. Although it was a great opportunity, Brad eventually realized he wanted a more significant career, and he called me out of the blue one day to talk about his future.

I was working as a college scout at the time, and he seemed intrigued with my work and thought he might enjoy working as a scout, too. By the next day, I had his resume and interviews set up with my company. We hired him a few weeks later, and he continues to be a rock star scout, evaluator and mentor with my old company many years later.

Even though he never got to play for me, his persistence in maintaining his relationship with me ended up leading to a great career and a great financial income for him. We still talk at least once per year, and I could not be prouder of the man he has become and the friendship that we have.

I want every family reading this chapter to keep Brad's story in the back of their minds. Brad cared about his relationship with me even though he didn't choose to attend my university. He had faith in the fact that I cared about him as a person more than I cared about what he could do on a basketball floor. The faith we had in each other led to a friendship that we are both very happy to have today.

As we continue to think about persistence throughout this journey, keep in mind the power of leverage and the power of creating and maintaining relationships. Every relationship built now could lead to a huge opportunity in the future when you least expect it or when you most need it.

A College Coach's Perspective

One of the biggest misconceptions I hear as a Head College Coach or when I am serving as a college scout recruiting for other coaches and programs is that coaches are only looking for the most talented kid. The truth is, we are looking for the hardest working kid and the kid with the most potential.

The best way for a student-athlete to demonstrate their potential is to commit to training out of the organized practices, watching film of yourself and others, and making sure you are eating right and getting the necessary amount of sleep to let your mind and body recover.

In short, separating yourself from competition means training when no one is watching. Study and learn your craft better than anyone else. Set yourself up for success with a disciplined lifestyle that includes rest and a healthy meal plan to allow you to be mentally and physically prepared.

Rebecca Begley

- 21 Years as a Head College Field Hockey and Lacrosse Coach

- 7 Conference titles

- 7 NCAA National Tournament appearances

- 3x Conference Coach of the Year

- 3x All-American student-athlete

Chapter 10: Action Steps

- Create a new set of goals each month. It may be as simple as increasing the 10 push-ups each night to 15 or 20 for the next month.

- As you are inviting four to five coaches each month to recruit you, find time at the end of the month to follow up with coaches who responded to you and those who did not respond to you.

- Make sure no month goes by without adding new and updated information to your on-line profile.

Chapter 11:
Apply and Visit

o———————o O o———————o

*If I was going to be successful, I had to be successful with myself.
I couldn't be successful doing what other people were doing.*

- Jay-Z

Can you see the finish line? You should be seeing the end of your journey at this point. You are almost there. You've done all the hard work, and it is time that you begin to understand the logistics necessary to close the deal.

At this point, college coaches should be communicating with you, and you and your family should feel like those relationships are getting close to an offer. Coaches are going to begin completing their processes to make sure you are truly a good fit for them. They've re-watched your film, called your coaches, invited you to visit, received feedback from their current roster if you visited, made sure you are academically a good fit, and they are deciding if and when they are going to offer you a roster spot and/or scholarship.

There won't be anecdotes or stories to tell anymore. The only story that is important from here on out is your story, and the last two chapters are designed to ensure a significant and happy ending!

ACT and SAT

I'm going to tackle the application process by asking you first to disregard anything you have read or been told about the ACT and SAT. Most of what you know about needing the ACT or SAT to apply and get accepted to college was for non-athletes, and that information will only hurt you if you continue to follow those guidelines and timelines. You are a student-athlete. You are on a completely different journey, and your rules are different.

High schools typically offer the practice ACT or SAT (PACT, PSAT) early in the first semester of the junior year and the actual exam in the second semester of junior year for a couple of key reasons:

1. Your high school administration understands that most kids will only take the ACT or SAT one time. They typically only offer one of those tests and not both. They choose the one your State Department of Education has recommended and what the public colleges and universities in your state require. Because of this, they want those kids to have as many high-level classes as possible and a good practice exam under their belt before they take their one shot at it.

2. If non-athletes take the ACT or SAT in May of their junior year and don't score well, they have the summer to take ACT/SAT classes or get tutoring in order to re-take

the exam in September or October of senior year and still be able to improve their scores before having to apply to schools in October and November of senior year.

As I have mentioned throughout the playbook, college coaches start evaluating potential recruits as early as the 6th grade. D3 and NAIA coaches can call prospects on the first day of their freshman year and can, theoretically, make scholarship (NAIA) and roster spot (D3) offers at that point.

Some D1 and D2 coaches can make verbal offers at any point, even to a middle schooler. D1 and D2 coaches can begin making scholarship offers in the summer between sophomore and junior year. If you wait until late junior year to take your first ACT/SAT exam, you are putting yourself in a position where coaches who are ready to make an offer based on your athletic ability may make that offer to another recruit because of concerns that you may not test well enough to be admitted to their school or that you may not perform well enough to be NCAA or NAIA eligible. College coaches simply don't want to take the chance on making you an offer when they aren't sure they can get you into school.

My advice, therefore, is to skip the practice exam and focus your time and energy on preparing for and taking the ACT and/ or SAT as a freshman or sophomore and then re-take the test at least two additional times (unless you test well and hit your goals on your first or second take). Colleges don't care how many times you take the tests. They are only focused on your *best* score and will disregard your first or worst. Taking the *actual* tests (not practice) multiple times early works to your advantage to not only be able to improve your scores but also for the opportunity to get noticed, recruited and offered sooner. [The only reason I recommend taking the PSAT is for the potential of earning a National Merit Scholarship. If you are a great test taker, this can be a significant opportunity to earn the chance to apply and earn the National Merit Scholarship.][9]

It does not typically matter which test you take. The reason there are two different tests (ACT and SAT) is because kids simply learn differently. One test (SAT) can sometimes be better for left-brained, analytical, STEM-centric kids, and the other test (ACT) can sometimes be better for right-brained, intuitive, creative, free-thinking kids. I recommend recruits take each test once. Whichever test they score better on or simply feel more comfortable taking is the one I would have them take a few times. All colleges and universities have a conversion table, so they know how your ACT score converts to the SAT and vice versa.

If I have not said it enough, I will make it clear here: **College coaches only have so many roster spots and so many scholarships. When their roster is full and the scholarships are gone, there is nothing left for you!** Whichever test you take, be the early bird, and you won't regret it. You can hop on-line right now and find test centers close to you and register for a test in the next 30 to 60 days. Typically, you must register a month in advance. Don't be afraid to invest in a good tutoring program for the ACT or SAT. Parents, if you could spend $500 for a six to eight week tutoring program for your child, knowing they could improve their ACT from

---

9   Claybourn, Cole, *"4 Reasons Your PSAT Scores Matter,"* U.S. News, *https://www. usnews.com/education/best-colleges/articles/reasons-your-psat-scores-matter (published November 9, 2022)*

a 21 to a 24 or improve their SAT from a 900 to an 1,150 while increasing their annual academic scholarship by $4,000 to $8,000 each year of college, wouldn't that be a worthwhile investment?

Next College Student Athlete (NCSA) states on their website that there are four reasons to take the ACT/SAT[10]:

1. Top-tier academic schools want to see your scores early

2. Getting recruited doesn't mean you're automatically accepted into a college

3. It may increase your chances of securing an academic scholarship

4. Adding a test score to your [on-line] profile can help you stand out

And I will add a fifth reason:

5. The NCAA will require all NCAA Division I and Division II student-athletes graduating in 2024 (post-COVID) and beyond to have passed the minimum requirements to be eligible to compete in their sport and/or receive an athletic scholarship.[11]

Don't underestimate the power of your ACT/SAT scores. Take your standardized tests early and often, and it will be the best gift you can give yourself for your athletic and financial future.

10   *NCSA College Recruiting, NCAA Eligibility Center - Sliding Scale, https://www. ncsasports.org/ncaa-eligibility-center/ncaa-sliding-scale#:~:text=Completing%20 the%20ACT%20registration%20or%20SAT%20registration%20process%2C,- doesn%E2%80%99t%20mean%20you%E2%80%99re%20automatically%20 accepted%20into%20a%20college*

11   *NCSA College Recruiting, NCAA Eligibility Requirements for Student-Athletes, https://www.ncsasports.org/ncaa-eligibility-center/eligibility-requirements*

College Application Process

Believe it or not, students can begin submitting applications to some colleges and universities as early as July heading into their senior year. I'll keep reminding you that you are a student-athlete and not just a typical kid applying to schools. You have a huge advantage in the recruiting process that a non-athlete does not have. You have a college coach who very much wants you on their roster. Where most non-athlete families go through the application process on their own, you will have a knowledgeable, experienced and sometimes powerful voice to help you apply and get accepted to your school of choice that the average applicant will not have. It is important that you ask the coach recruiting you to give you their recommendations on such things as:

- How and when to apply

- What to write in the application essay (don't be afraid to ask the coach if they can read your essay and give you feedback before you submit it)

- Knowledgeable college staff and alumni to speak with before applying

- What the application deadlines are and if you have any wiggle room with those deadlines as a sport recruit

For a student-athlete, this may be the easiest part of the entire journey if you lean on your new coach to guide you through the process. If they do not offer their support and guidance, make sure you ask for it. A good college coaching staff knows the ins and outs of the admission process on their campus better than anyone else. They can't and won't apply for you, but they can show you the most efficient ways to do it right, so you get your desired result: ADMITTANCE!

Financial Aid

Even though Financial Aid was originally intended for those who needed it most, it actually goes to those who know the most about the process. In the world of college athletics, there is nothing worse than going through this long, arduous process to get recruited by a great coach with a great program at a great school, only to then find out your family cannot afford to accept the offer. I can think of 10 student-athletes right off the top of my head that I loved, who wanted to choose me and my program, but who, in the end, couldn't accept my offer because of the cost. In this section, I want to provide you with the steps to take so that you can greatly decrease the chances of that happening.

STEP 1: Early investment

Start saving NOW! The sooner you start saving money for college, the more you can grow it, making it that much easier to pay for college. Below are some growth options I recommend researching, especially the 529 Plan in your state. There are financial advisors around every corner. I won't pretend to be an expert, but my wife and I started contributing to a 529 Plan when our first child was born, and it is the best investment we have made for our children's futures. By sometimes contributing as little as $50 per month, we will have enough saved to be able to pay for most of both of our children's educations when they graduate from high school. Again, do your research, but I recommend asking a financial advisor to give you their advice on why, when and how to use the 529 or to recommend a better option for you:

- Interest-based savings account
- Money markets
- CDs/Bonds
- 529 Plan
- Many other options…refer to your financial advisor

STEP 2: Academic achievement

Your grades and test scores will affect your total scholarship and financial aid more than anything else. Why?

- The better your grades, the more money the college will give you in academic/merit scholarship.
- The more academic scholarships you receive, the less the coach must give you in athletic scholarship, and therefore the more attractive you are to that coach.
- You want to be a Mercedes the coach can get for the cost of a Ford. By being a great student, the college gives you more money. Therefore, the coach gets a great player for much cheaper.

STEP 3: FAFSA—The Free Application for Federal Student Aid

Everyone should complete the FAFSA on-line.[12] Families can begin applying for federal student aid beginning on October 1 of a student's senior year.

---

12 *https://studentaid.gov/h/apply-for-aid/fafsa*

- The earlier you apply, the more grant money will be available.

- Once you have completed the FAFSA, you will receive an EFC (Expected Family Contribution) budget from the government. Based on your income taxes from the previous year, your EFC is what the government is telling colleges that your family can afford out of pocket and how much financial aid they can give you, which the government will reimburse them.

- The EFC helps the colleges/universities you apply to better understand what your family can afford to send **one** child in your family to college based on your household income. A college coach will often ask you if you know your EFC. That helps them understand what their school may end up giving you to offset tuition and room and board costs.

- The U.S. government gave out $246 billion in 2021-22.[13] What's heart-breaking is that $3.75 billion of that in Pell Grants alone went unclaimed.[14]

- Even if you think your family makes "too much," you should complete the FAFSA because you never know as a family when a parent might lose a job or a family's income might dramatically decrease from year to year. By not applying for aid, you may lose the opportunity to get the help when you need it most.

---

13   *College Board, "Trends in Student Aid: Highlights" (2022), https://research.college-board.org/trends/student-aid/highlights*

14   *Tretina, Kat, "FAFSA Income Limits 2023: Are You Eligible For Student Aid?" Forbes Advisor, https://www.forbes.com/advisor/student-loans/fafsa-income-limits/ (updated July 21, 2022)*

- EVERYONE who applies receives financial aid. When you receive your financial aid, you can accept it or decline it, but it is always nice to know what free money is available to you if you want it or need it.

STEP 4: Leverage and competition

- The more coaches that recruit you, the bigger the sense of urgency those coaches will feel to make you an offer. DO NOT limit yourself to just a few colleges or local colleges.

- When creating your college lists, make sure to focus on 10+ schools at every division level. Each school will have their own financial aid structure, and you want to find out your best fit but also where you can maximize your financial aid.

- If NO one is recruiting you, you have ZERO leverage for the coaches to take you seriously OR to offer you anything.

- If you have MULTIPLE coaches recruiting you, coaches must now compete for you and that puts you in the driver's seat. LEVERAGE!!!

STEP 5: Athletic scholarships

I have spent a lot of time writing about how college coaches can and will use athletic scholarships, but the bullets below should help organize those thoughts.

- College athletic scholarships are very tough to come by. Over 80% of the college scholarships given each year

DO NOT come from NCAA Division I schools. NCAA Division II, NAIA and the NJCAA schools give out four times more scholarships than NCAA Division I schools.

- NCAA Division III schools are NOT allowed to give athletic scholarships, but they will work hard to meet your financial need with financial aid, merit and academic scholarships, and institutional grants.

- NCAA Division I, II schools and NAIA schools are able to give full-ride scholarships based on your athletic ability. NJCAA can give full-tuition scholarships. Room and board scholarships are few and far between at the NJCAA level.

STEP 6: Private scholarships

- While many private scholarships and community service scholarships may only award a few hundred dollars, this money can help you pay for books or living expenses.

- Research your local businesses and community organizations to find out if they give an annual scholarship and what qualifications and application processes are required.

- For those of you who want to pursue a career in medicine, business, education, engineering, etc., after college, I recommend taking a hard look at Volunteer Scholarships.[15]

---

15   Barge, Mary Ann, SAT / ACT Prep Online Guides and Tips - The Complete List of Community Service Scholarships, https://blog.prepscholar.com/community-service-scholarships-complete-list (published November 12, 2022)

Visits

Visits are the stage where a coach really likes you, and you really like them. They want you to visit their school, and you want to find out if the school makes you feel as good as the coach has made you feel.

You have talked with the coach and have chosen a good day and time that works well for both of your schedules. Now what? You need to focus on three steps for your visit: (1) Preparing for the visit, (2) What to accomplish on the visit, (3) What to do after the visit.

Step 1: Preparing for the visit

Research the college/university's website:

- Confirm they have your major and classes listed for your degree path

  o Ask the coaching staff if they can set up a class visit in your major while you are on campus.

  o Write down questions you want to ask a faculty member and the coaching staff about registering for classes, balancing your grades and team commitments, and how it works when there is a conflict with classes and practices.

- Review their admissions and financial aid standards and write down questions:

  o Ask the coaching staff if they can set up time to meet with both an Admissions and Financial Aid representative while you are on campus.

o Think about your family's situation and income. Does your family own their own business with lots of expenses and overhead? Is one or more of your parents out of work? Are one or more of your parents active or former military? Are you financially supporting a family member who is living with you, like a grandparent whose expenses do not show up on your taxes? Write down questions you want to ask the Admissions and Financial Aid staff. Having considered these questions, you will be better prepared for the questions they will ask of you.

- Review the community at-large:

  o Where is the nearest airport/bus station/train station?

  o Can freshmen have cars on campus?

  o If freshmen can't have cars, is there public transportation to get around town?

  o Are freshmen required to live on campus?

  o What are the demographics of the student body?

  o Is there a religious affiliation? Are you comfortable with their views and requirements?

  o Who is the University President? Who is the Athletic Director? How long have they been there? What are their philosophies? What have they accomplished in their tenure?

- Questions to ask of the Head Coach or Assistant you are working with before the visit:

- o Can you have an overnight stay in the residence halls with one of the returning players?

- o Can you have time to eat at least one meal with the team in the cafeteria, preferably without the coaching staff? (Don't tell the coaching staff this, but you want time alone with the players without the coaches around, so you can get the player's unfiltered opinion of the school and coaches.)

- o Can you have time to watch a practice or game/event while you are on campus? If they are out of season, ask if you can watch an open gym or a workout. Depending on the sport, there may be an open gym they can put together, so you can play with the team while there (i.e., basketball, volleyball, soccer).

- o What should you bring with you? (I.e., transcripts, letters of recommendation, potential NCAA or NAIA paperwork, etc.)

- o What should you wear and pack for clothing/shoes?

Step 2: What to accomplish on the visit

- Enjoy yourself. Have fun. Imagine yourself being a student on that campus.

- Spend as much time with the team and the coaches as you can. Do you like them? Do they like you? Can you see yourself with these people for the next four years?

- Ask the members of the team questions:

  - o Why did they choose the school?

- o Are they happy with their decision?

- o Do they like the coaches?

- o Do they feel the coach was honest with them when recruiting them? Has it turned out as they expected?

- o Do they have any advice for you?

- Ask the coaches questions:

    - o Would you mind watching some of my game footage with me?

    - o What do you see as my strengths and weaknesses?

    - o What do you like about my ability that fits your team?

    - o What are your strategies and philosophies for next year?

    - o How do I fit in with the returning team members?

    - o If you offer and I accept, am I guaranteed a Varsity roster spot?

    - o Do you have any scholarships remaining (if D1, D2, NAIA or JC)?

    - o Do you see me as a scholarship-level player today (if D1, D2, NAIA or JC)?

    - o What is the process if I get sick or hurt during the season?

    - o How do you view the balance between Academics and Athletics? What processes do you have in place to help with class scheduling, academic progress reports, tutoring, and keeping me on track to graduate in four years?

o How many recruits are you planning to recruit in my class?

o What is the roster size you like to keep for the program?

o What type of relationship do you like to have with your athletes?

o Do you have an open-door policy?

o Do you provide the players with your personal cell phone number?

o Do you prefer my day-to-day needs to come straight to the Head Coach or the assistants?

o What does long-term support look like? (I.e., helping with internships, alumni relationships, job placement, etc.)

o Do you provide financial support if your players want to work on their post-graduate degree while there?

o Would I lose my scholarship if I were to have a season or career-ending injury or illness?

Step 3: What to do after the visit

- Once home, sit down and write down the pros and cons of your experience while they are fresh on your mind.

- Nothing is too small or too big. These are the next four years of your life. Write down all the good and the not-so-good that you heard and experienced. You are going to want to make visits to three to five different schools. Your pros and cons list for each school will be important in Chapter 12.

- Send the coaching staff a hand-written thank you note. It is possible they made you an offer while you were on campus. One way or another, you want to make sure you show your gratitude for asking you to visit

What is the difference between an official visit and an unofficial visit?

Any visit to a college campus by a college-bound student-athlete or his or her parents paid for by the college is an official visit. Visits paid for by college-bound student-athletes or their parents are unofficial visits.

What if you receive an offer while on the visit?

The key is to expect the worst and prepare for the best before you go (yes, I meant to say it this way). If the offer comes, great! Take a deep breath and thank the coach for the amazing honor. Tell the coach that your family has made a commitment from the beginning of your recruiting journey that you were going to talk through every step together and make sure to think through every opportunity before making any decisions.

"Coach, I am thrilled with the offer, but would you be comfortable giving us time to discuss the offer as a family? When would you need a final answer from us?"

What if you have more visits set up and are expecting offers from other schools that may be a better fit or you just don't feel like you are ready to commit?

The above response will work if you have more visits set up. Try never to give the coaching staff more information than they need to know. Feel free to re-phrase the questions above with:

"Coach, I am thrilled with the offer and cannot thank you enough for thinking I am worthy of playing for you. However, my family has committed to a process from the beginning of my recruitment, and we have a few boxes to check before we are prepared to accept an offer, including a couple additional visits we have scheduled. We want to make sure we see all our options, so we have confidently learned everything we need to make a good decision. Our last visit is on _____. Would you be comfortable giving us until _____ to give you our final answer?"

We will dive more into the commitment process in the next chapter, but I want you to be prepared for any situation before it arises.

A University President's Advice

I enrolled as a freshman in the first and only college I ever visited in fall of 1987. I moved into a residence hall larger than my hometown. My first class was bigger than my entire high school. It was overwhelming and I graduated four years later. Although I am a proud alumnus, I wouldn't suggest that anyone model their college search process after mine. My wife and I have spent the last 30 years in higher education, much of it in admission and financial aid, and our expertise was put to the test this past year as our son and daughter (twins) decided on their respective colleges. Both included athletics as a significant variable in the decision process. One is attending a large public NCAA Division I institution, the other a small private NCAA Division III institution, and I believe they each made the right decision.

I appreciate you have been given a lot of advice, tactics and recommendations in the preceding pages. Below you will find five questions that can be modified to fit the person answering them — parents, grandparents, family, high school student, or college transfer. I encourage you to answer them as sincerely and as honestly as possible and discuss your answers with invested parties.

How do I make decisions? *The decision of where to go to college is highly personal. Trust the process. If you are a list maker, make lists. If you are a person who makes major decisions on feeling and intuition, walk the campus and trust yourself.*

What do I want in a college experience? *The average student is in class for 15 to 18 hours per week and there are 168 hours in a week. What you wish to study is important; however, considering 90% of your time will be spent doing something other than attending class, it is imperative you assess how your expectations of college fit the institution.*

If I decide to change my program of study, are there enough options to explore without switching schools? *It is estimated that 20% to 50% of students enrolled undecided and more than 50% of students change their major at least once. Enroll at an institution that provides enough flexibility to grow, evolve and possibly change your mind.*

Are there family considerations whether, spoken, assumed, or implied? *Our daughter eliminated a school because I said I would never wear a shirt with the school's mascot on it. As a student-athlete she wanted me to be proud of her alma mater and to proudly represent her and her teammates. I was shocked to learn*

I was the reason she eliminated a school. Talk about it. Decide who gets a voice and who gets a vote. Ignore the opinions of everyone else!

Will my peer group support and encourage my success? *Our son had an unbelievable academic, athletic and financial package at an institution. He decided it was a great opportunity, but it was not the right opportunity for him and he was right. We are naturally influenced by our peer group. Consider whether your peers will pull you toward commencement, athletic success, maturity, and a life of meaning and value. If you are less than confident in the people you will be immersed with at a specific college, keep looking.*

Dr. Rich Dunsworth, President of the University of the Ozarks

Chapter 11: Action Steps

- Apply for three to five schools that are actively recruiting you. If the coach is not recruiting you, don't waste your time or money applying...unless you are willing to give up playing and are okay just being a student at a school.

- Apply for the FAFSA as early as possible. Remember, you will have to apply for federal aid each year, not just your first year.

- Visit three to five schools whether your dream school and dream coach are making you an offer or not. Make sure you've given yourself the opportunity to compare. You will feel much better about your final decision if you know you have completed the process of looking at other campuses.

- Take your first ACT or SAT by the end of sophomore year, and then re-take one or both exams as often as you feel comfortable. Often, just by re-taking the exam a few times, your comfort level will increase, and your knowledge of how to move through the exam and what to expect can greatly improve your scores.

Chapter 12:
Commitment—Close the Deal

*In life you make the small decisions with your head
and the big decisions with your heart.*

- Omid Kordestani

We have finally come full circle. Our conversation started with understanding and developing your commitment to the process, and we are now finishing our journey with your commitment to your school of choice.

This is the most rewarding part of our journey but is not a step that can be taken lightly. This is often where the biggest mistakes are made. In this final chapter, I am going to explain a lot of terms and phrases that you will encounter or that you may be interested to learn how they affect you. Again, the more you know and the more prepared you are, the better your decisions will be.

I am going to take you backward a couple of steps before we move forward because it is easy to get confused with what the word "offer" really means, and I want to make sure you understand how to handle each type of offer that may come your way. There are many different types of offers…too many to go into in this chapter, but I will focus on the big five: Verbal Offer, Financial Aid Offer, Walk-on Offer, Preferred Walk-on Offer, National Letter of Intent (NLI).

Verbal Offer

A verbal offer is a **non-legally binding scholarship offer**, and college coaches can extend verbal offers to a recruit of any age. Think of a verbal offer as someone giving you an engagement ring. They are serious about you, but the ring does not mean you are legally married. It is simply a statement to commit to wanting to get married. You or the person who gave you the ring can back out of that commitment all the way to the altar and right before either of you says, "I do."

It is imperative that you ask good questions once that verbal offer is made. In the prior chapter, I taught you how to handle a verbal offer during a visit to buy yourself some time to think through the offer, so you are not caught off guard on your visit. However, most offers will be made over the phone. **Here are a few questions to consider asking the coach once the offer is made:**

- Have you made any other verbal offers to recruits in my class?

- Have any of those recruits accepted your verbal offer?

- How many returners plus incoming recruits that play my position do you expect to have on the roster my freshman year?

- How many commitments do you expect to get in my class?

- Are there any other recruits you are making an offer to who compete at my position/event?

- Have you ever pulled a verbal offer from a recruit? What were the reasons?

- At what point does this verbal offer become a binding offer between you and I? What is the timeline for that decision?

- Are there any scholarship dollars attached to this offer?

Financial Aid Offer

Many of you will receive offers from NCAA D3 schools. Those schools cannot offer you scholarship dollars based on your athletic ability. NCAA D3 schools cannot offer you an NLI or National Letter of Intent, so you will <u>not</u> have an official Signing Day if you decide to play at the D3 level. What you will receive from D3 schools, instead of the NLI, is a Financial Aid Offer. This will be a written document that will either be mailed or E-mailed to you once you have applied for Admissions and Financial Aid from the school. This document will include, but will not be limited to:

- Academic scholarship
- Institutional grants/scholarships
- Federal grants (i.e., Pell)
- Private scholarships
- Student loans
- Parent loans
- Work study

When you see pictures of D3 recruits on Signing Day, they are either signing a blank sheet of paper or their Financial Aid Offer. It's a great picture, but it is all for show.

If you decide to sign this financial aid offer, it is still not a binding agreement between you and the coach, but it basically tells you both that you are committed to each other. D3 coaches will exhale with great relief when a recruit signs their financial aid offer. It is clear that the coach wants you on the team in some capacity, and you have decided you want to attend this college/university and play on the team in some capacity. The coach can still cut you from the team at any point or ask you to play on the JV team, but that is why you always want to ask the questions from the Verbal Offer section above before putting your signature on anything.

When you do sign your Financial Aid Offer, you are agreeing to pay the remaining costs after accepting the school's financial aid options. (Understand there are many ways to pay off the balance. Always ask for alternative options if the costs are more than expected.) You don't have to accept everything they include in the offer. You may want them to eliminate part or all of the loan options, and/or you may not be interested in accepting the work study option. That is 100% up to you. The school is going to give you everything they can to make the costs of their college/university cheaper for you and your family while attempting to get your total costs down to your EFC (Expected Family Contribution), as we discussed in Chapter 11.

NCAA D1, D2, NAIA and JC schools can and will provide you with a Financial Aid Offer as well. Some divisions, sports and schools will want you to walk-on or may only be offering you a partial athletic scholarship. The only difference at the non-D3 schools is that they can add a partial or full-athletic scholarship to your Financial Aid Offer.

Walk-on Offer

A Walk-on is basically an offer to come to their school and try out once you get there. The coach likes you and your potential, but they are not willing and/or able to offer you athletic scholarship dollars or guarantee you a spot on the team. They are simply giving you the opportunity to prove your worth and earn a spot on the team.

Every year, ESPN and other news outlets will post inspirational videos of walk-ons earning a scholarship and the team celebrating that student-athlete's accomplishment. These are few and far between. That is the risk versus reward proposition you are taking by accepting a Walk-On Offer. It is up to you to make the most of it. If you want to see an entertaining version of how challenging the walk-on process can be, I encourage you to watch the film *Rudy*. The dedication and commitment you must make to turn your walk-on dreams into a scholarship reality is very clearly depicted in this film. It's also a great motivator for any student-athlete who is questioning their personal commitment.

Preferred Walk-on Offer

These are typically going to come from D1 college coaches. With a Preferred Walk-On Offer, there really is no difference from a traditional walk-on. When a coach provides a *preferred* offer, they are basically saying "We really want you on the team.

We are giving you a guaranteed spot on the varsity roster, but we do not have any athletic scholarship to give you this year."

If you watch any D1 Football, Basketball or Volleyball on TV, you are typically seeing at least one if not multiple preferred walk-ons on every bench. It became more prevalent during the COVID years because many seniors lost their final year to the pandemic, and the NCAA gave those kids an extra year of eligibility. That means a lot of incoming freshmen lost their scholarship and were asked to be preferred walk-ons for a year with the understanding that they would get their scholarship in Year 2 once those seniors finished their extra year of eligibility.

Preferred offers are typically better than a normal walk-on offer, but you are taking the same risks by taking that offer. There is nothing binding or written, and the coach can change their mind at any point.

National Letter of Intent (NLI)

NLIs are the Mount Everest of offers. You may be an exceptional athlete with amazing ability, and a D1 coach gave you a verbal offer at a camp you attended as a 7th grader. That offer means nothing until you sign your NLI. NCAA D1 and D2 programs all have different days and times when they can send you an NLI, but it will typically be your senior year beginning in early November. That NLI must be sent through the mail, so you will a get a hard copy to review and sign in your mailbox, and you must return it in the same manner in often a very short window of time.

The NLI is the only offer that locks you into that college/university with an athletic scholarship offer to play for that team. I took the below information straight from the National

Letter of Intent website, so you fully understand the parties at play and why it exists:

The NCAA manages the daily operations of the NLI program while the Collegiate Commissioners Association (CCA) provides governance oversight of the program. Started in 1964 with seven conferences and eight independent institutions, the program now includes 652 Division I and Division II participating institutions.

The NLI is a voluntary program with regard to both institutions and student-athletes. No prospective student-athlete or parent is required to sign the NLI and no institution is required to join the program.

The NLI is a binding agreement between a prospective student-athlete and an NLI member institution.

- *A prospective student-athlete agrees to attend the institution full-time for one academic year (two semesters or three quarters).*

- *The institution agrees to provide athletics financial aid for one academic year (two semesters or three quarters).*

The penalty for not fulfilling the NLI agreement: A student-athlete has to serve one year in residence (full-time, two semesters or three quarters) at the next NLI member institution and lose one season of competition in all sports.

An important provision of the NLI program is a recruiting prohibition applied after a prospective student-athlete signs the NLI. This prohibition requires member institutions to cease recruitment of a prospective student-athlete once an NLI is signed with another institution.[16]

---

16   http://www.nationalletter.org/aboutTheNli/index.html

Basically, what this last part means is that once you sign your NLI, all the other schools who have been recruiting you must stop contacting you. You are legally married. No one can ask you on a date anymore…metaphorically, of course. The NLI is the only offer that expects true commitment, respect, and integrity by all parties. Most college coaches run their programs with those values as the centerpiece of their program, but the NLI helps the NCAA enforce those values for those schools and coaches who may happen to live in the grey areas of recruiting.

Choosing the Right School

Now that you have a better idea of the type of offers you may receive, it is important that we talk about choosing the right school. A recruit may only receive one offer, but it is very likely that if you have followed the process of this playbook, that you will have multiple offers from which to choose. How do we determine which offer to take?

I recommend going back to Chapter 4 and Chapter 11 and combining your priority questions and answers with your post-visit pros and cons into a document that gives you a clear breakdown of how you feel about all the schools that have made offers to you. Something like this:

PRIORITIES	SCHOOL A	SCHOOL B	SCHOOL C
Course of Study (Majors)	x	x	x
Distance from Home	x		x
Preferred Climate		x	
Size of School	x		
Student-Teacher Ratio	x	x	x
Family Budget			
Demographics	x	x	
Culture	x	x	
Head Coach	x	x	x
Coaching Staff	x	x	x
Present Roster		x	x
Play Right Away		x	x
Style of Play		x	x
Quality of Degree	x	x	x
Facilities	x		x
Pros	*Only two hours from home *Great internship programs *Coaches seem to really want me *Love the new residence halls and athletic facilities	*Love the warm weather/close to the ocean *Loved the people and culture *The coaches and players were great *Coaches seemed to really want me *Fits our family budget (full tuition paid)	*Only three hours from home *Loved the professors I met and classes I observed *Real chance to start right away *Had the most fun with the players on the team *Nationally ranked program the last three years
Cons	*Cold winters *Most expensive school of Top 3 *Play is slower than I like *Didn't click with a lot of the players *I may have to sit a year or play a bench role in Year 1	*Furthest from home *Plane ride every time I want to go home *School is really small *Facilities are older and seem a bit run-down	*Cold winters *2nd most expensive of the 3 schools *A little concerned about the surrounding areas of the city - campus is not in a great part of town *Very little diversity on campus

As you are considering your options, it is extremely helpful to have everything you have learned and experienced in one place. The flexibility of having this document printed or on your phone allows you to read it, consider it, make changes and adjustments, and clearly evaluate your options.

Within a few hours or a few days of reviewing your chart, I recommend that you begin to rank the priorities on the left from top to bottom. After your visits and reviewing your pros and cons, you may find that the things that were initially your top priorities are now closer to the middle or bottom of your list and vice versa. Good visits will and should affect your priority list. You are going to learn things about yourself that you did not expect.

The biggest challenge in making a good decision is finding out what your most important needs and priorities are. Use this chart to figure out what is most to least important. You may find yourself deleting or adding categories that I have not presented. Listen to your heart. Have lots of discussions and positive debates. In the end, I think this chart will end up being your best friend. My hope is that your family will start using this type of process for all your big decisions: picking a new house, taking a new job, buying a new car, or even choosing your next vacation destination. Have fun with it, and I am confident good will come from having it as a tool for your family.

The Final Commitment

You did it! You have received an offer (or offers) and you've made the commitment to your school of choice! Congratulations! I could not be happier for you and your new coach. It's been a crazy ride, but I hope it has been fun and you've learned a lot while learning a lot about yourself.

Below are some tips to follow before you move to campus.

What to do after verbally committing to a coach and program?

- Stay connected. Make sure there is an open line of communication between you and the coaching staff. Make sure you understand who to call when you have questions throughout the transition process to campus.

- If you live in a two- to three-hour radius of campus, I encourage you to make some additional visits to campus when and if you can. Go practice with the team or go watch them compete live if they are still in season.

- Start talking with the other recruits and returning members of the roster. Start building friendships and learning the ins and outs of the program. Your new coaching staff will provide you with their contact information.

- Ask your new coaching staff for their out-of-season workout regimen. Start doing the conditioning and strength training they will ask of you as soon as you can start.

- Keep your focus on your grades. When you commit you will probably still be in high school, so continue to focus on maintaining or increasing your grades. Remember, the habits you have built in high school are going to pay major dividends when you get to college. Don't let those habits and routines slide. Now is the time to make them a more consistent part of your life.

- Stay out of trouble. Remember John's story in Chapter 9. Just because you are committed, doesn't mean your situation cannot change.

What to do after you have signed your Financial Aid Offer or NLI:

- Work with your new coaching staff to finalize the following:
  o Housing and roommate situation
  o Class schedule
  o Summer opportunities to play against college-level talent
  o Summer camp coaching opportunities
  o Opportunities to watch film from previous season
  o Opportunities to start studying next season's playbook and team philosophies

A College Coach's Advice

My advice for any student-athlete and their families…..

Find a happy place!

After the visits, application process and acceptance letters, narrow your list down to a few places that you feel the best about. Once you have your few schools that you could see yourself at, do it all again! You need to ask for what you want. Ask the coaches to meet again in-person or virtually. If they really want you, they will do it. You need to gather as much information on the team environment as you can. The only way to do that is to communicate with the coaches and current players. Ask to meet with the team, go to as many contests as you can, and follow the teams on social media. This will help give you a picture of what their environment is like. In order for you to improve and be the best athlete you can be, you need to be in a situation that you enjoy. That doesn't mean it will be easy. The best coaches will always challenge you to exceed your potential.

I have seen many athletes over my 25 years of coaching who didn't choose the best situation for them. There are many reasons this happens. Sometimes athletes jump at the first offer. Sometimes athletes are pressured into a situation and are afraid it will go to someone else. Most of the time, student-athletes don't get enough information. Information is power. The more you know, the better the decision you can make for your future.

The combination of a dedicated student-athlete, a powerful and impactful college athletic program, and a rigorous academic experience will make the path to a successful career in sport and/or life possible.

Go find your happy place, and you will find your success!

Mark Murphy

Head Women's Tennis Coach, Kalamazoo College

- 2X NCAA DIII Regional Coach of the Year
- Coached 17 All-MIAA First Team selections
- Coached 13 All-MIAA Second Team selections
- Coached 5 MIAA MVPs

Chapter 12: Action Steps

- Put together your Pros and Cons chart after your visits.

- Listen to your gut—which school and experience has motivated you and excited you the most?

- Don't think about the alternatives. If you are going to commit, go all-in. Focus on making the absolute most of the decision you've made!

Final Thoughts

It has been my pleasure to share my stories and knowledge that I have gained over the years with you. From the beginning, my goal in writing this playbook was to help families put the power of playing in college in their child's hands. In the introduction, I talked about removing the word success from your vocabulary and replacing it with significance. As we complete this journey, my hope is that the lessons learned can and will be used long after your recruiting journey is over.

I want every teenager to have a better understanding of their own value, their self-worth, and the difference between "what I want" and "what I need."

My hope is that the next time your family has a big journey or a big decision ahead of you, you can come back to <u>Significant Recruiting</u> and pull ideas to help you with any obstacle, problem or opportunity you may be facing.

In the end, I am thrilled if you truly feel like the CEO of your future. You didn't wait around hoping someone would find you. You didn't have to settle for the only coach who recruited you. You didn't find yourself dropping out of college or jumping from college to college because you did not know how to ask the right questions and demand the right answers before making life-altering decisions.

Now it's your turn. Keep being curious. Keep striving for significance. I wish you and your family all the best, and I will be cheering for all of you. Go make your dreams come true!

Acknowledgements

I owe a tremendous amount of gratitude to my book coach and friend, Cat Margulis. If not for her, I would still be re-writing Chapter 1. Thank you, Cat, for your guidance, motivation, honesty and significant coaching. Not only do I have a book I am extremely proud of because of you, but I am also confident that I have many more in me to write. I would play on your team any day!

Thanks to Quinn Wirth and Brad Butler for helping me dig through the slog of titles and giving this book its long-awaited name while also letting me share your stories with others. However unique our journey was to finding each other, I am forever thankful for your friendship and your generosity.

Thanks is not near enough for Coach Jerry Petitgoue. My high school coach never wanted much to do with me, so to have one of the greatest of all time take me under his wing all these years is a blessing I don't think I will ever be worthy of. I am forever thankful for your mentorship and support. Karen and I are eternally blessed to call you and Joan our friends.

Huge thank you to my coaching brethren Lori Chalupny Lawson, Caleb Lawson, Mark Edwards, Chris Krich, Dave Kaneshiro, Rich Reed, Oliver Wiseman, Chris Bunch, Samantha Birkicht, Rebecca Begley and Mark Murphy. You have all graced me with your more than generous contributions to this playbook. You have all made such a significant impact on my career in ways you can't imagine. I am a better man and coach by being able to watch the way you impact the lives of your student-athletes. I am forever thankful for your friendship.

Thank you to Dr. Rich Dunsworth for being my lighthouse during my darkest days. Your friendship has never wavered in over 25 years, and I am confident that you are a big reason why my best days are still ahead of me.

Thank you to Dr. Jim Phifer, Dr. Keith Lovin, Dr. Beth Triplett, Dr. Larry Hays, Mr. Rich Fanning, Mr. Gene Myers, Mr. David Clark and Mr. Chris Hickenbottom for never giving up on a young man many, many years ago who had a ton of potential and very little discipline. I continue to strive each day to be the leader you hoped I would become. Thank you for continuing to define significance for me.

Thank you to Jeri Strohecker, Wendy Bashant, Bob Drexler and Gina Hausknecht for helping me find my love of writing and guiding me to what I was meant to do. I am sorry it took 30 years for me to figure it out!

Thank you to all my present and former players at Whitfield School, Maryville University of St. Louis, the University of La Verne, Douglas County High School, Castle View High School and D'Evelyn High School. I know I didn't always live up to my quest for significance with all of you, but I am so thankful that I had the true pleasure of coaching you. It has been one of my great joys in life watching you become the men and women, husbands and wives, loving fathers and mothers, and great teachers and coaches so many of you have become. I love you, and you are forever my family until the end of time. I got your back!

Thank you to the men and women who have had the great challenge of being my assistant coaches throughout the years. Your time, dedication, and love for our players is much more than I deserved. I will forever be thankful for your patience and friendship.

Thank you to my 14 nieces and nephews who suffered through having an uncle not much older than them as he tried to figure out how to be the best version of himself. You were the best guinea pigs a young coach could ask for. I am so proud of all of you for who you have become in spite of having to put up with me. And, thank you for making me a Great Uncle 21 times over. I love you all more than you know!

Thank you to Tim, Beth, Bobby and Sue for being the best big brothers and big sisters a boy could ever ask for. If I have made any significant impact on the lives of others in this world, it is because of the love and support you have given me since the day I was born.

Thank you to Ken and Margaret Numoto (and Karissa and the entire Numoto-Tabuchi clan). I thought I hit the jackpot when your daughter said "Yes" to my marriage proposal after only six months of dating. To be blessed with a 2nd Mom and Dad like you has been a dream come true. Thank you for your warmth, generosity and always being there when we needed you most. I am the luckiest guy on the planet to have all of you in my life. I know Margaret is looking down from the heavens with a giant smile on her face.

Thank you to my mom and dad, Greg and Rosemary Rogers. You made sure that respect, hard work, empathy, tolerance, humility, generosity and faith were not just words to me. You gave me a foundation of significance that has enabled me to be a brother, uncle, teacher, coach, husband, father and son I hope you can be proud of. I am proud to be your son, and I am thankful for every day I have with you. I love you both!

Thank you to Kaia and Kade for putting up with a daddy who decided to have a midlife crisis in the middle of your most important years. Thank you for your patience, love and support while I have been writing this book these past few months. It is more than I could ask for. I love you more than all the planets and the stars and all the universes.

Finally, thank you to love of my life, Karen. I love you more each and every day. I cannot imagine life without you. You have been my best friend for 26 years, and I can't wait for all the trips and adventures we have yet to take.

Want More Coach Rogers?

If your family, school, club or organization would like to schedule Coach Rogers for 1-on-1 or group recruitment advising, motivational/educational speaking, or you are just looking for more detailed direction and support for your recruitment needs, you can find his recruiting services and more on his website at www.significantcoaching.net or by clicking the QR Code below. Any thoughts, questions or feedback can be sent to Coach Rogers at coachsignificance@gmail.com. I look forward to hearing your personal story of significance!

About the Author

Matt Rogers is a 26-year veteran high school and college coach, administrator and scout. He has led two teams to the NCAA National Tournament and helped lead another to a High School State Championship. His teams hold numerous school records and one NCAA record. He has mentored and coached players at every collegiate level while serving as an athletics administrator at the high school and NCAA DII and DIII levels. Over 25 of his players have gone on to be high school and college coaches. For nine years, he served as a National Speaker and Head Scout at NCSA where he helped over 4,000 student-athletes around the world achieve their dream of playing their sport at the college level. Coach Matt presently lives in the Denver, Colorado, area with his wife and two children.

Made in the USA
Columbia, SC
31 August 2024